ENGAGING

IMAGINATION

in ECOLOGICAL EDUCATION

Practical Strategies for Teaching

Gillian Judson

Pacific Educational Press
University of British Columbia

Engaging Imagination in Ecological Education: Practical Strategies for Teaching

Published by Pacific Educational Press
University of British Columbia

Publisher: Susan Howell
Managing Editor: Katrina Petrik
Developmental Editors: Theresa Best, Barbara Kuhne
Production Manager: Elizabeth Salomons
Production Editor: Nancy Wilson
Indexer: Stephen Ullstrom
Designers: Sharlene Eugenio, Mauve Pagé

Cover photographs: (front) ©iStock.com/da-kuk; (back) ©iStock.com/KatarinaGondova

Every effort has been made to identify copyrighted material, obtain permission from copyright holders, and credit sources. We will gladly correct any errors or omissions in future printings.

We acknowledge the financial support of the Government of Canada through the Canada Book Fund (CBF) for our publishing activities.

LIBRARY AND ARCHIVES CANADA CATALOGUING IN PUBLICATION

Judson, Gillian, author
Engaging imagination in ecological education: practical strategies for teaching / Gillian Judson.

Includes bibliographical references and index.
Issued in print and electronic formats.
ISBN 978-1-926966-75-5 (pbk.).—ISBN 978-1-926966-76-2 (epub).
—ISBN 978-1-926966-77-9 (mobi).

1. Human ecology—Study and teaching. I. Title.

GF26.J83 2014   304.2071   C2014-904744-4
                                          C2014-904745-2

Printed and bound in Canada.

20 19 18 17   3 4 5 6

Ella and Chloë Judson,
two of my most inspiring teachers

Contents

ACKNOWLEDGEMENTS

I would like to acknowledge the sources of knowledge, guidance, wonder, and inspiration that have contributed to this book—these are my teachers. I owe an immense amount to Dr. Kieran Egan, my mentor, colleague, and friend. Kieran, you have forever changed my understanding of learning and teaching. Due to your guidance, honesty, humour, and unwavering support, I have grown as a thinker, writer, and teacher. I am also very grateful to Laura Piersol, Michael Derby, and Jodi MacQuarrie. Our conversations have inspired me. I am personally and professionally changed as a result of talking with you, observing your reflective practices, and reading your thoughtful musings, papers, and poetry.

To my parents, Claire and Ed Dyatt, I owe the greatest acknowledgement of all. You provided me with a magical childhood, instilling in me the ability and desire to see the wonder and mystery in the world around me. Extra thanks to you, Dad, for your careful editing—you spent countless hours reading and rereading this text for nothing more than the odd coffee in payment!

Last but not least, I want to acknowledge a different, though no less inspiring, teacher: the natural world. Through my involvement with the Maple Ridge Environmental School Project, I had the great opportunity to immerse myself in the forests and parks of Maple Ridge, BC. The lessons in this book have their roots in my emotional engagement in a particular place, and my openness to experience what the natural world has to offer.

INTRODUCTION

What's it got to do with me, Ms. J? There I stood, empty water bottle in hand, giving a student the evil eye. How many times had I asked my students to recycle their plastic water bottles? I felt extremely frustrated—why didn't he put the plastic bottle in the blue recycling bin? Lack of knowledge was not the problem. Every classroom in the school had recycling bins; most businesses and homes have them as well. It is widely acknowledged that recycling is one way to reduce humanity's impact on the planet. In effect, recycling is one practical aspect of a broader interest in transforming the ways in which people interact with the world around them. It is one doable piece of a much larger agenda to make human beings more aware of their role in protecting the planet's environment. So I was not talking about an isolated school initiative; rather, it was a pressing social issue that has become a pervasive dimension of the educational agenda in nearly all schools.

As students bolted for the door and I looked with some dread at the towering pile of unmarked assignments on my desk, I pulled the empty bottle from the garbage can—which was situated *right beside* a very large, very blue recycling bin—and called the student back. I asked him, "Why didn't you recycle this bottle?" Usually students squirm a little and quickly offer a sideways apology: "Right! Sorry. Forgot. Oops." This time my student didn't apologize or make an excuse. Instead, he asked me why he should bother: "What's it got to do with me, Ms. J?"

This student expressed a sense of emotional disconnection from a situation much larger than himself, much greater than one plastic bottle ending up in the trash rather than a recycling bin. This was a good, conscientious student who, like many others, was gaining knowledge about ecological issues in school and society at large, but who felt little, if any, personal connection to these issues. I observed in this student, at that moment, an expression of disaffection—a feeling that I've sensed with my students before and also, at times, within myself. Is recycling a bottle really going to make a difference? Why bother? It is becoming increasingly clear that our survival as a species requires more than recycling; it requires reimagining humankind's relationship with the natural world.

I am not the only one to notice a disconnection between knowledge and action.[1] Despite knowing what is going on and going wrong in the world, human beings continue to have little to no emotional connection to it and little to no commitment to do anything about the effect our collective actions are having. It seems, however, that the people who are most concerned about the earth—who are committed to making significant lifestyle changes for the sake of all life on the planet—have an emotional and imaginative connection to the natural world that runs very deep. Often, but not always, this is connected to engagement with the natural world in childhood.[2] Teaching in ways that afford students opportunities to *feel* something for what they are learning, by engaging their bodies, emotions, and imaginations in the world around them, is what this book is all about. It answers a question that teachers are increasingly seeking to address: What is required to educate for ecological understanding?

Overview

This book is designed for educators who want examples of what students' emotional and imaginative engagement in learning and in the world around them looks like in practice. It also provides resources for lesson and unit development and addresses issues such as assessment and implementation. It is a practical guide for teachers of students of all ages and in all contexts—urban, suburban, and rural—who are seeking to educate for ecological understanding. To understand ecologically is to make sense of the human world as part of, not apart from, nature; it is to understand humankind's "implicatedness in life."[3] If we are to reduce our impact on the earth's natural resources, a deep cultural change is required to make long-lasting changes in the ways that we choose to live our lives.

Ecological understanding represents a radical shift away from the industrial mindset that has set humankind apart from nature and has also fuelled much of human development in the Western world. Ecological understanding requires reimagining ourselves and our world based on emotional and imaginative engagement. What this means in practical terms is that our beliefs and actions as a species will be influenced in no small way by a deeply felt connection with the world around us. There's a slogan in my daughter's elementary school classroom that reads "From Me to We." It is a call for greater social responsibility, reminding children to be inclusive and embrace the diversity of the human community in which we live. Ecological understanding could use the same slogan, although with a much broader embrace. The "we" now includes the natural world, and our thinking about how to live is profoundly influenced by this realization. Thinking "we" engages social and ecological responsibility simultaneously. Emotional and imaginative connection to the local natural and cultural context in which people live supports the kind of care and concern for the earth that underlies more harmonious human action and decision-making.

For educators, cultivating ecological understanding is a much more challenging task than imparting knowledge of ecological issues—something that still tends to dominate some ecologically oriented educational programs.[4] Educating for ecological understanding requires focusing on engagement throughout the teaching and learning process. Emotional and imaginative engagement with knowledge, with the world, and with the local natural and cultural contexts in which our students live and learn can support the kind of decision-making and action that addresses significant aspects of consumer-oriented cultures. For example, we should wisely *refuse* first, then reduce, reuse, and recycle. With ecological understanding framing the ways in which we make sense of our world, we may see more reusable water bottles and fewer plastic ones. We may also see less paper in recycling bins, *not* because it has been thrown in the trash, but because we have radically reduced the use of paper. In short, recycling is important but it simply isn't enough. If we happily recycle but do not question the underlying issue of how much we consume and what impact our consumption has on the earth, then we are not going to be able to make the radical decisions—and changes—required to support a sustainable environment and healthy planet.

The chapters that follow provide a description of key principles of an approach to teaching called Imaginative Ecological Education (IEE).[5] This method of teaching is centrally concerned with student engagement with knowledge and with the natural world of which students are part. You will read about how students can develop literacy skills through teaching that engages them as trackers in nature. As they learn to read signs in the natural world around them, they will also learn to read the symbols of alphabetic literacy. A unit on weather situates knowledge associated with science, social studies, and mathematics curricula within a context of students training to become meteorologists. Indoors and outdoors, IEE encourages students to feel, honour, collect, and organize knowledge about the various forms of weather around them. Through these examples, you will see how to replace the industrial model for teacher planning with a socio-cultural conception of learning that provides you with tools for making knowledge meaningful in students' minds.

Chapter 1 provides a critique of current programs in ecological education and explains the rationale for implementing an Imaginative Ecological Education program. Chapter 2 provides an introduction to the theory of IEE and its three principles: *Feeling, Activeness,* and *Place*. These principles are then discussed in detail in chapters 3, 4, and 5. Chapters 3 and 4 use a unit on weather to illustrate how the principles can be translated into practice. My hope is that you will find that the tools I employ with the topic of weather can be used to shape numerous other topics that you teach. Chapter 5 focuses on place-based activities that enable students to develop a *sense of place* and *feel* something for the contexts in which they live. The detailed examples in these chapters illustrate how curricula can be designed using tools of the imagination and how, as a result, educators can cultivate ecological understanding as part of everyday teaching.[6] Chapters 6 and 7 provide a unit on teaching literacy—a topic that some readers may not immediately consider imaginatively engaging or conducive to ecological teaching. These chapters address the question: "How do we teach children to read and how do we develop literacy skills in imaginative and ecological ways once students can read?" Chapter 8 reviews the practical dimensions of IEE, addresses implications for assessment and evaluation, and includes resources for getting started, collaborating, and implementing IEE in schools and classrooms.

IEE is not a new curriculum. It is an approach to teaching any curriculum—and any age of student—in a way that engages the body, emotions, and imagination in the process. The chapters that follow provide you with the needed background knowledge and resources to use this approach in your teaching.

CHAPTER 1

THE RATIONALE FOR IMAGINATIVE ECOLOGICAL EDUCATION

Do we really need *another* educational program? Aren't there plenty of educational programs available to the school districts, schools, and teachers taking on sustainability initiatives? Unfortunately, there aren't. For the reasons that I will address below, this chapter addresses why, for the most part, the educational programs and resources currently available are ill suited for cultivating ecological understanding. They are imparting knowledge but ignoring the emotional and imaginative core of ecological understanding. Consequently, students' behaviours often do not change—as illustrated by the example in the introductory section of this book, where a student did not bother to recycle his plastic bottle.

The Limitations of Current Ecological Programs

I am hardly the only one suggesting that humanity should care more about the earth or that teaching should cultivate students' ecological understanding. If you look at the mission statements of many schools, you will likely find references to the social need to address ecological issues and to create more ecologically aware citizens. In most mainstream schools, however, the interest in encouraging students' sense of ecological responsibility is one of a wide range of social and academic goals that include, for example, the development of social responsibility as well as increased literacy and numeracy skills. It is rarely acknowledged that cultivation of ecological understanding is an aim that requires a different pedagogical approach from the objectives-based model currently shaping educational practices.

In mainstream schools, teachers may connect curriculum topics to the natural environment in their local areas from time to time, possibly offering some outdoor and hands-on learning in attempts to get students outside.[1] Students in these schools may also have the opportunity to participate in immersive types of ecological educational programs. There are many different education centres, programs, and schools that describe themselves as "ecological," "place-based," or "environmental." When funding is available, they may offer immersive, ecologically oriented experiences for students that aim to develop ecological understanding. (For example, a quick internet search for such programs close to my home found S.E.E.C.—the Saturna Ecological Education Centre on Saturna Island, British Columbia, Canada.)

There are also ecologically oriented public schools that make the cultivation of ecological understanding of more central importance. Examples include Sunnyside Environmental (Middle) School in Portland, Oregon, and the Coombes School in West Berkshire, United Kingdom.[2] In attempts to connect children to nature, some public schools have made pedagogical changes that are even more radical. In these schools—often considered alternative—there are no school walls at all. The natural world is the classroom. In the last few years in North America, for example, there has been an increasing interest in fully outdoor, nature-based schooling for young children. These kinds of programs have been around for much longer in the UK and other European countries, and are serving in some cases as models for North American programs.[3] Under the names of "Forest Kindergarten," "Nature Kindergarten," or "Outdoor Kindergarten," the concept of fully outside learning for young children is beginning to take its place in the range of educational program options available in North American school districts.

For example, both the Cedarsong Nature School (in the state of Washington) and the Mother Earth School (in Portland, Oregon) offer outdoor kindergarten programs. The Cedarsong Nature School has been offering nature immersion programs since 2006 and, more recently, a fully outdoor kindergarten program. The Mother Earth School, which first opened in 2007 with a single kindergarten class and is now enrolling students in kindergarten to grade 2, combines the Waldorf educational philosophy with a place-based learning model.[4] In Canada, the Equinox Holistic Alternative School, founded in 2009 and located in Toronto, began offering an outdoor public kindergarten education program in the 2012–2013 school year. In British Columbia, outdoor primary education programs are being offered in various school districts, including Sooke and the Sunshine Coast. Since 2011, an entire elementary school curriculum has been taught "without walls" in the outdoor spaces of Maple Ridge, BC. In multi-age groups, students in kindergarten to grade 7 have been using the parks of Maple Ridge to learn the curriculum. My work on IEE as a curricular approach stems, in part, from my work with this project.[5]

A teacher recently told me that her school was implementing the "West Coast recess"— that is, no matter the weather, kids spend one recess per week outside. While I am not sure how far this particular initiative can move us towards ecological understanding (it seems more likely that we will need to learn to deal with dripping kids), it does reflect a broader acknowledgement of the value of children spending time outdoors. My research shows, however, that an increased interest in getting kids outside and interacting with nature is not necessarily for the primary purpose of increasing ecological understanding. For example, Knight defines the Forest Schools movement as follows:

> In the UK, Forest School is a way of working in an outdoor environment, preferably but not exclusively in wooded settings. This is based on the premise that repeated enjoyable outdoor experiences will have a positive effect on people, including on their potential dispositions for learning or for personal change…[6]

Knight's account of the rise of Forest Schools in the UK and the diverse program offerings within this field[7] demonstrate how this initiative is based on the belief that learning in the outdoors supports students' personal growth and their physical and emotional well-being. Similarly, both Constable and Slade, Lowery, and Bland describe the ethos and primary aims of Forest School programs in terms of increased motivation and engagement, development of creative and critical thinking skills, and social, personal, and emotional well-being.[8]

In the outdoor education movement one also finds that the cultivation of ecological understanding is not necessarily a central pedagogical aim. Allen Hill describes the "contested space of outdoor education" in which issues of "identity, philosophy, theory, curriculum, and pedagogy" continue to be discussed.[9] He acknowledges that, more often than not, outdoor education is not aimed at developing ecological understanding; instead, many outdoor education programs in the Western context reflect the primary aims of adventure pursuit and personal development. Hill believes, however, that outdoor education should attend more specifically to ecological concerns, and he has designed a model that interconnects the aims of outdoor and sustainability education initiatives.[10]

Not surprisingly—and thankfully, from my perspective—it seems outdoor learning experiences, no matter the intent, can increase students' understanding of, and feelings of connection to, the earth. Two studies of student experiences in Forest Schools—by Ridgers, Knowles, and Sayers and by Slade, Lowery, and Bland—indicate how these programs increased students' knowledge of the natural world,[11] and their "understanding and appreciation of the natural environment,"[12] despite the fact that students did not acknowledge increased care and concern for nature to be a primary aim of the program.

The dual aim of these programs to get students outdoors and increase their contact with nature aligns with Richard Louv's argument that human beings *need* nature.[13] That is to say, a primary rationale for moving learning outside—or, at least, increasing the number of experiences children have outside—revolves around the benefits nature can have for human health and well-being. The interest in connecting people with nature to evoke a more fundamental change in human-nature relationships is not discounted, but it is *not* the driving force behind these initiatives. Rather, we hear the argument that human beings are increasingly suffering the consequences of living in an urban, indoor, plugged-in world. This kind of thinking reinforces instrumental values of nature—preserve nature because we can use it and need it to survive and thrive—rather than acknowledging the value of nature for its own sake.

I do not disagree with Louv's thesis that human beings' psychological, emotional, and physical health stems, in part, from contact with nature and that nature does people good.[14] But a human-centred rationale for reimaging our relationship with nature won't take us far in shifting our perceptions of the world and our place in it. IEE builds on the premise that nature is *intrinsically* valuable, not only because its preservation appears crucial for human flourishing. Indeed, the kind of profound shift in human thinking required to address ecological issues is not possible if we continue to think about nature's value in instrumental terms. If we are to resolve local and global environmental crises, it is necessary to redefine the human-world relationship.[15]

I expect that many people considering nature-based experiences for children will find Louv's arguments compelling.[16] It is natural for people to want to do things that are beneficial for their well-being. Personal needs aside, however, it seems to me that the earth desperately needs human beings with an emotional connection to nature that translates into a desire to live differently. If we are healthier as a result—and no doubt we will be—that is a bonus.

There is a subtle difference between Louv's views and the premise behind adopting IEE as a pedagogical approach. Therefore, providing a rationale for IEE is crucial. Unless teachers see the importance of a new educational approach to ecological education, the effect they have on developing their students' ecological understanding will be limited. What I hope to show is that we will not be able to reimagine the human-world relationship without a pedagogical approach that

- centralizes ecological education in the curriculum;
- gets students outside;
- recognizes the importance of human beings' emotional and imaginative nature as crucial to shaping understanding and behaviour; and
- situates learning in the natural and cultural contexts in which students live and learn.

Supplemental, Infusionist, and Intensive Approaches

Currently, the resources available to teachers that make ecological education integral to the curriculum are limited. Most of the resources available today leave ecological education as an "add-on" to the curriculum or are tied to a specific subject area. This supplemental approach offers teachers curricular materials in the form of self-contained teachable units or lesson plans (for example, Project Wild materials or resources available through a magazine such as *Green Teacher*). In an infusionist approach, ecological topics or themes are used to shape particular curricular areas (such as social studies or language arts). In an intensive experience approach, students spend a few days once—or, if they are lucky, twice—in a school year at an outdoor education centre or program where they are immersed in nature-focused curricula. An example of this approach is the Sea-to-Sky Outdoor School for Sustainability Education, located in North Vancouver, BC. In all three of these types of programs, ecological education remains peripheral to students' learning.

Changing the Context

Currently, students are primarily learning indoors. If we adhere to the belief that *real learning* takes place at desks or most certainly within school walls, we cannot change students' understanding of the world around them. We have been so conditioned to think about learning in particular ways that we don't question the negative impact that staying indoors might be having on student learning and student understanding of the world. I am suggesting that long-held and unquestioned classroom routines—how topics are taught, how we expect students to demonstrate learning, and even the programs we offer—may be stifling student imagination. We need to bring novelty into learning by changing the learning context—in this case, through relocating learning—but also through new, imaginative forms of engagement.

Consider also that if we assume that the classroom is the site of real learning, we may be contributing negatively to our understanding of ourselves as a species. The fact that we continue to separate ourselves from the world around us in order to learn about it is indicative of the ways we conceive of our relationship to the world. Imaginative ecological education addresses these negative features of current practice by getting students outside classroom walls more frequently and as part of the process of learning the mandated curriculum.

Technology and Ecological Education

You may be wondering how technology fits into ecological education. Can some of the high-tech graphics and high-definition forms of media support the development of ecological understanding? Learning about nature inside rather than outside is a lot like conducting a music class without instruments or song. It is one thing to talk about playing a trumpet or singing and quite another thing to actually do it. While television and classroom teaching can provide knowledge, they cannot replace the awareness and emotional attachments that develop from direct experience in nature.[17] In order to be able to emotionally and imaginatively engage with the natural world—to develop a connection with the diversity of life that surrounds them, no matter where they are in the world—students need to get outside. It is outside classrooms and school walls that students will more routinely experience their connection with the natural world around them, whether by feeling the breeze on their arms or the warmth of sunshine on their faces. An imaginative and ecological approach to teaching will challenge the norms and routines of classroom teaching, engaging children in learning within the world they inhabit. In rural, suburban, and urban contexts, imaginative ecological educators will extend their classrooms into the natural and human communities around them.

What Sets IEE Apart?

What differentiates IEE from the many models and programs currently used for ecological education is that it takes into theoretical and practical account the fact that students are emotional and imaginative beings. If we take this into consideration, it becomes obvious that the kinds of objectives-based models shaping our pedagogical practices are in many ways ill suited for the task. As Egan convincingly argues, teachers are often unaware of the theoretical bases shaping what we do in schools.[18] That is, we take for granted many pedagogical practices that are actually products of some dubious theories from the past that today do not deliver the assumed educational benefits. We are unfortunately living a legacy in which an industrial type of metaphor has been applied to our thinking about how best to teach. The assembly line of the 1920s was a great advance for industry, but I question the appropriateness of this particular metaphor for thinking about how to teach human beings.[19]

The legacy of thinking of teaching in industrial terms permeates teaching practice to this day, despite widespread acknowledgement of the inadequacies of such a metaphor for education.[20] We can still, in many ways, liken unit and lesson planning to a factory process. The efficiency of it appeals to us, as does the logic of the linear approach.[21] Contradictions abound, however. The notion of "efficiency" as it is used in production doesn't go far when it comes to developing human minds. Moreover, there are many limitations to taking a complex topic—whether it is literacy, numeracy, or any current event—and identifying a step-by-step way to teach it.

Pretend for a moment that you are a fly on the wall of a typical staff room. You will hear discussion of the frequently unpredictable nature of classroom learning, the diversity of students' interests and abilities, and the need for differentiated learning to address this multiplicity. You will also hear teachers discuss their planning and practice in standardized and objectives-based terms. Objectives-based models, influenced by Tyler,[22] are assumed to be useful for any teacher, anywhere, to shape any knowledge into a potentially meaningful learning experience. We advise new teachers to add to an objectives-based model a concern for student diversity and recognition of the myriad factors that define good teaching. Here is the standard recipe: begin with Tyler's objectives-focused pedagogy; add an openness to engage flexibly in the curriculum process by involving students and their diverse needs and interests, as well as parents and colleagues; then add a well-defined lesson or unit outline based on prescribed learning outcomes that are clearly articulated; and *voilà!*—one is ready to teach.

I question the common assumption that educators can teach according to a conception of the mind and intellectual development that neglects imagination. That is, we continue to think about planning in an overly industrial, standardized way. An objectives-based rationale has forced emotional and imaginative engagement onto the sidelines, as "hooks" or "frills," rather than recognizing this as being at the heart of learning. How does knowledge become meaningful if not through emotional attachment in the human mind?[23]

Marginalization of emotion and imagination in learning is particularly problematic in the context of ecological education, where the goal is not only to teach students about the world around them, but to do so in ways that leave them *feeling* and inclined to *do* something about the current state of affairs.

Imagination plays at least two roles in ecological understanding. On the one hand, imagination offers the possibility to transcend current understandings of the world and consider alternative possibilities.[24] Although taking on different names in the literature, such as empathy,[25] inclusion,[26] or identification,[27] imagination seems to play a role in enabling us to take on alternative perspectives.[28] For ecological education this represents an important step towards establishing a new path for human interaction with, and human conceptions of, the earth.

On the other hand, emotional and imaginative engagement is the glue that bonds us to the world. Our emotions are one of the central ways in which we make meaning, orient ourselves to our world, and make sense of our experiences. For students to feel part of a living world, we must engage their emotions and imaginations in learning about it. In the context of ecological education, our pedagogical approaches to date—based largely on an unquestioned objectives-based model—fail to acknowledge how they are mismatched with the goal that they aim to achieve. In short, the current means and ends of ecological education practices are misaligned.

The neglect of emotion and imagination in education is paired with a failure to acknowledge and engage the body in learning. The kinds of activities students are engaged in during current ecological education programs are not necessarily contributing to their sense of connectedness with the natural world. For students in mainstream schools, simply being outside or doing activities outside will not necessarily contribute to their sense of connection to nature.[29] One way to address this disconnect and to increase students' feelings of connectedness with nature is to design activities that engage the body. The body is, of course, one of the primary means through which we make sense of the world around us. We are born with tools for "sense-making" that include the body's senses, but also emotional response, a sense of pattern and musicality, and a sense of the incongruous. We are not mere "thinkers"; David Krech coined the term "perfinkers" to indicate how we perceive, feel, and think together. Unfortunately, common pedagogical theories do not acknowledge us as such and therefore educators too often conceive of students simply as minds, rather than recognizing that they have embodied minds and that learning is a process that always involves knowledge, perceptions, and emotions.

In order to support ecological understanding, the activities students are doing and the ways they are being taught must engage their bodies, emotions, and imaginations with nature.[30] Failure to activate students' emotions and imaginations in learning may limit the extent to which they can form personal relationships with the earth. This is a major shortcoming of current programs: imagination has had a surprisingly negligible influence in the shaping of ecological education theory and practice.

Unless teachers opt to connect their teaching to the local context, the particularities of the places in which they are teaching may not enter into the topics at hand. So, presumably, an objectives-based unit planned in Memphis can easily be used in Manitoba. Why? Because place—the natural and cultural contexts in which we live—has nothing to do with what is being taught.

The Benefits of IEE

Given the limited teaching time and resources most teachers have, you may wonder if it makes sense to integrate place into all that is taught. How, for example, would one teach a historical topic such as World War I or a mathematical concept such as the Pythagorean theorem in a place-based way? More to the point, is it worth the effort? While I am not suggesting that every topic should connect to place, I am inclined to think that if teachers *did* consider place when they plan everything they teach, they would enhance their teaching and open up greater possibilities for student engagement. Currently, place-based dimensions are not on most teachers' radar. But there are aspects of all topics—themes or principles, for example—that students can investigate in relation to the local context in which they live. Teachers can afford students opportunities to situate their understanding and build the emotional connections to place that underlie ecological understanding by asking: "What does this topic mean *here?*"[31]

From an ecological perspective, the "placelessness" of curriculum planning is detrimental to learning. Some of the world's greatest wonders lie at our fingertips if only we are mindful of their existence. By ignoring place we ignore the wonder in the world around us that can engage our hearts and minds in learning. In ecological education programs, teachers are encouraged to connect to the natural and cultural worlds in their local areas—but how? This is where current approaches fall short. There is little indication of how engagement in place can be incorporated centrally in all teaching. Moreover, there is little indication of *how* students actually use their imaginations and emotions to make sense of the places in which they live.

The pedagogy described in the following chapters makes the development of ecological understanding part of everything students learn. Through opportunities to learn outside, in direct contact with nature, and by participating in activities that involve the body, students' emotions and imaginations may be engaged in ways that support them in developing an ecological understanding of their world.

CHAPTER 2

PRINCIPLES OF IMAGINATIVE
ECOLOGICAL EDUCATION

Imaginative Ecological Education is centrally concerned with cultivating relationships. It is a distinct application of relational pedagogy. This focus on relationships is what sets ecological education apart from related educational programs such as, for example, environmental education, environmental learning, place-based education, and education for sustainability.[1] Smith and Williams describe how ecological education emphasizes the "inescapable embeddedness of human beings in natural systems."[2] In practice, ecological education "requires viewing human beings as one part of the natural world and human cultures as an outgrowth of interactions between our species and particular places.... There is no way to disentangle human beings from the earth, and as long as our species exists, no way to separate the earth from humans."[3]

Like teachers in other environmental education programs, IEE teachers strive to make cross-curricular connections. They work to develop students' sense of participation in human and natural communities and encourage their students to be thoughtful about their impact on the planet. But in IEE, much more pedagogical attention is focused on cultivating students' emotional and imaginative relationships with knowledge and with place.

In IEE, ecological education is always linked to the field of imaginative education.[4] By reconceiving ecological education along the theoretical and practical lines of an imagination-focused approach to teaching, the idea of relational pedagogy is transformed. Now, in addition to the inter-human, community-building relationships inherent in relational pedagogical practices in schools[5] and the kinds of human-nature relationships that ecological education includes, IEE adds the emotional relationships with the knowledge in the curriculum and the natural and human learning contexts. IEE supports the cultivation of meaningful relationships in education by employing learning tools that tap into students' imaginative lives. By using learning tools such as the story form, mental imagery, and the extremes and limits of reality, students can *feel* something for the topics in the curriculum and the places where they are living and learning. So, for example, students may learn about single-celled organisms in a way that encourages them to appreciate the tenacity of these astonishing entities. They may finish their study of soil with a sense of the mystery of life and death it contains, or finish their unit on worms with a respect for the great strength and vulnerability of these creatures.

Three Principles of Engagement

Feeling, *activeness*, and *sense of place* are the three principles of engagement for educating for ecological understanding. Each has associated with it learning tools we can use in engaging students' emotional and imaginative lives (see table 1). This chapter provides a brief overview of these three principles, which will each be given more theoretical and practical detail in subsequent chapters.

While recognizing that our emotional and imaginative lives can't be so easily put into boxes as table 1 might suggest, this chart outlines the tools that I discuss throughout this book. These learning tools are tied to the body and to the different forms of language that we employ, allowing us to conceive of learning in imaginative and emotional terms. By using these tools to shape our teaching, we acknowledge that human beings are emotional and imaginative beings. From the outset, our educational means and ends are aligned.

Weaving as Metaphor

As I briefly introduce the main principles of IEE, visualize imaginative ecological educators as weavers. They weave relationships that connect knowledge, the body, and the natural and cultural contexts. They also weave wonder into the everyday experience of students in schools. Like any metaphor, thinking about teaching as weaving has its limitations. Nevertheless, I think it can contribute to understanding what is distinctive about IEE as a pedagogical approach. Weaving requires mindfulness in interconnecting warp and weft. Imaginative and ecological teaching requires mindfulness in interconnecting students with knowledge and place. Weaving also requires artistry; each cloth is a work of art that reflects the diversity of the context in which it was created. Like Eisner, I believe there is a degree of artistry in good teaching that we tend to forget amidst ongoing drives to standardize curricula and universalize the educational experience of students.[6] Weaving, as metaphor, reminds us of some of these often forgotten dimensions of teaching.

TABLE 1. IEE—PRINCIPLES OF ENGAGEMENT AND COGNITIVE TOOLS OF THE IMAGINATION

FEELING		ACTIVENESS	SENSE OF PLACE
Some Tools of Oral Language—Mythic Understanding	Some Tools of Written Language—Romantic Understanding	The Body's Tools	Place-Making Tools
the story form	narrative structuring	the senses	the sense of relation
binary opposites	heroic	emotional response	formation of emotional attachments
metaphor	qualities	gesture	
jokes and humour	sense of wonder	sense of incongruity and humour	creation of special places
mental imagery evoked from words	humanizing meaning	sense of pattern and musicality	
rhyme, rhythm, and pattern	extremes of experience and limits of reality		
sense of mystery and puzzles	collecting and organizing		
games, drama, and play	the literate eye		
	change of context and role play		

Feeling: The First Principle

Homer was a weaver. He was a weaver of tales.[7] The story was Homer's tool: it stitched together the events described and the feelings of those who listened. We are all, to lesser degrees, storytellers like Homer. We are all weavers of tales and, whether sitting before an attentive audience or not, we shape the events of our lives in story form. The story is one of the most powerful means human beings have to convey meaning. The gift of story is something all human beings gain when they learn an oral language. The story tells us how to feel about the events that make it up. "How was your day?" Answer this question in any detail and you tell a story. "What do you do for work? Tell me your story." What the story form offers the human mind, then, is a learning tool. It ties up our emotions with the events that are recounted, enabling us to more readily remember the contents of the story.

Everything we teach can be shaped in story form. Imaginative ecological educators, as storytellers, do not view the curricula as simply bodies of knowledge but, rather, as good stories to tell. This does not mean creating fictional accounts for the topics they are teaching; rather, teachers think about their topics as reporters would. For example, reporters ask questions before writing news stories to determine *the story* on any given topic. When we identify the story, we are identifying the emotional core of a topic. By shaping our teaching in a way that brings this emotional core into focus, we engage our students' emotions in learning. One way to teach about water in story form is to engage students' sense of wonder with its permanence: There is simply no way to get rid of it.

The story form is one of many cognitive tools that help us to learn and make meaning in the world around us (see table 1). It, like other cognitive tools that include mental imagery evoked from words, jokes and humour, and transcendent or heroic qualities, is a cultural invention that helped our ancestors make meaning of their experiences. Like all other cognitive tools, it makes knowledge memorable by evoking emotion and imagination. Over time these cultural inventions have become conventions of language so that as we learn language—first oral language and then written language—we encounter a wide variety of these tools. Cognitive tools make up the toolkits of our imaginations. They help us to think, and are the means by which students can begin to *feel* something for all aspects of the curriculum they are learning. Imaginative ecological educators shape their teaching plans around the kinds of cognitive tools their students are already using to make sense of the world. This approach enables educators to create imaginative contexts for their students and brings wonder into learning.

Activeness: The Second Principle

Have you ever felt frustrated when students seem to perpetually forget to bring materials to class? Whether they forget books, paper, pens, pencils, rulers, or calculators, our students seem to forget materials we deem important for learning. It is also the case, however, that educators seem to have forgotten that when students come to class, they *do* consistently come equipped with a powerful set of learning tools that are part of the body. These learning tools include the physical senses (smell, touch, hearing, sight, and taste), emotional responses, a sense of humour, musicality, and the ability to perceive patterns. These are the body's tools that engage students' imaginations in the world. Do our lessons actively incorporate these tools? IEE requires tapping into the body's emotional and sensory tools in learning. Topics are learned in ways that weave together the body's understanding and its perception of the world around it. Lessons that incorporate imagination engage students as perceiving, feeling, and thinking beings.

Activeness, as distinct from the concern with "being active" that is most commonly seen in schools, requires more than simply doing things. Activeness is not kinesthetic learning. Rather, I use the term to refer to how engagement of the body's innate tools can contribute to learning by developing a distinctly body-based understanding of topics, whether students are learning about fractions, punctuation, or countless other topics. Activeness contributes to the cultivation of ecological understanding by heightening students' awareness of their bodies in the world. Through full sensory engagement of the body in the world and through the emotional responses this evokes, we may cultivate emotional connections with the world around us.[8]

Sense of Place: The Third Principle

Place and sense of place are concepts being discussed in multiple disciplines, including geography, psychology, sociology, architecture, and cultural studies.[9] Of course, each discipline uses the terms differently, so I will explain here their significance for IEE pedagogy and the cultivation of ecological understanding.

In a general sense, places are the meaningful contexts of human perception of, and participation in, the world.[10] They are meaningful because they evoke emotional response; we *feel* something about them. As we observe and participate in the activities of daily cultural life, and as we make sense of our experiences, the spaces where we are and the contexts we find ourselves in take on meaning.[11] Sense of place refers to how we understand and relate to these contexts. It is made of interconnected emotional and intellectual dimensions; it takes shape around what we feel about place and what we know about place.[12] Sense of place involves, thus, both a personal relationship with one's context as well as a certain depth of knowledge about it.

Typically, students know very little about the history or geography of the local contexts in which they live. Similarly, they may not have any particular feelings about the local contexts; that is, they sometimes don't have much sense of place. In mainstream schooling, beyond an interest in meeting certain mandated learning outcomes related to local history or geography, cultivating students' sense of place is simply not a priority. When the development of students' ecological understanding is a concern, however, engaging them with their contexts—that is, affording students opportunities to emotionally and imaginatively connect with the wonder of the world around them—is important.[13] Why? Because it is widely believed that, by supporting our students in developing a sense of place, we may create relationships that can support feelings of care and concern for the world.[14] IEE is different, however, from other place-focused programs. What sets IEE apart from other ecological programs is that it conceives of developing a sense of place in imaginative terms.

IEE is based on the premise that there are distinctive ways in which our imaginations develop a sense of place. In other words, just like we have access to cognitive tools that help us to learn and *feel* something for what we are learning, we also employ tools for developing a sense of place or "place-making."[15] For example, young children seem to grasp meaning in their contexts by forming emotional associations with features of their environments. These associations—whether to routines, objects, people, or animals—contribute to a sense of belonging and emotional connection. In IEE, educators can cultivate their students' sense of place by incorporating this tool in teaching. Young children can be given opportunities to "apprentice to place," for example, by returning over the course of a few months or a school year to a specific location in the schoolyard or a local park and keeping track of its seasonal changes.

For older children, opportunities to identify special places to call their own—forts and hideouts, for example—contribute to how they develop emotional connections to their contexts. This seems to be a feature of older children's place-making process. IEE educators will consider how students can explore their local environments as part of learning. For example, what patterns can be found in the everyday objects of the schoolyard? What is unique about IEE is that the emotional and imaginative core of sense of place is acknowledged in pedagogical practice. Whether IEE teachers are addressing mathematics, social studies, language arts, physical education, or any other curriculum topic, they tap into the imaginative tools that students are already using to grasp the meaning of the world.

Developing a sense of place takes time. In relation to this principle, IEE is a "slow" pedagogy. Those teachers fortunate enough to work in the places where they spent their own childhoods may already have developed a relationship to place. But for most teachers, time must be spent getting to know, enjoy, and "breathe in" the place where they teach in order for an emotional connection to develop. How many teachers work in the context in which they live? How many teachers, among those that do live and work in the same place, have emotional connections with it? How many teachers have time to develop a sense of place? This does not happen quickly or easily, which is perhaps why a more standardized approach to teaching still dominates the way we plan for ecological education.[16] But engaging with place is not an objectives-based process. It is an imaginative one and requires an imaginative approach. The time we spend cultivating our own and our students' sense of place is pedagogically valuable. Indeed, by engaging place-making tools we see how the particular place-based knowledge students are encountering with their emotions makes learning meaningful and memorable.

We see, thus, that three kinds of relationships are woven together in IEE. Each is woven through engagement of the imagination in learning. These relationships are woven in a school setting that emphasizes relationships. Which school doesn't work to develop a sense of community? Which school doesn't work to form partnerships between students, parents, teachers, administrators and, frequently, members of the wider community? Now, however, the notion of community extends beyond the human dimension. The application of an imaginative and ecological perspective to the process of building a sense of community makes IEE distinct. Learning opportunities that engage the imagination and that nurture students' sense of relationship with place aim to increase students' understanding of how they are part of both cultural and natural communities.

Identifying Sources of Emotional and Imaginative Engagement

As you examine each of the principles of IEE in turn, I invite you to consider what possibilities this approach to teaching can offer your students. I encourage you to try out the principles as you read about them. For example, as you read in chapter 3 about the cognitive tools of oral language, consider the story of whatever topic you will teach next. Think about the different ways in which the IEE approach might transform how you teach topics that don't appeal to you or your students. Consider how you could transform topics seemingly unrelated to the goal of developing ecological understanding.

Imaginative ecological educators begin by identifying their own source of emotional and imaginative engagement. Can you identify what is wonderful about what you are teaching on Monday morning? For many teachers who were once students—and now work—in Western educational systems that are thoroughly shaped by progressivist educational thinking inspired by Piaget and Dewey, it is unthinkable to suggest that we should focus on ourselves rather than on the students in our classrooms. I would argue, however, that until we focus on our own engagement—that is, until we identify within ourselves what attracts us to a topic—we are not going to be able to inspire our students. Every teacher knows that it is his or her own excitement about a topic that really engages students.

You will find two detailed examples of the IEE approach in this book. The first, a unit on weather—addressed in chapters 3 and 4—illustrates how the IEE principles of *feeling* and *activeness* might play out. Chapter 5 outlines how developing a *sense of place* can be implemented as you teach different curricular topics. While this breakdown of topics does not reflect how teaching is actually done, it is helpful for the purposes of illustrating the principles of IEE. The overall aim of the unit is to engage students' emotions, imaginations, and bodies with the weather. The weather isn't something we will understand in any meaningful way if we only look at it through a window. If we want a richer understanding, we need students to experience it, and perceive, feel, and think about it.

In chapters 6 and 7, a second detailed example of the IEE approach shows how a unit on literacy can be taught imaginatively and ecologically. I chose literacy for a few reasons. First, I genuinely wondered how one would teach students to read and write in ways that focused on imaginative and emotional engagement of the body. Second, I was intrigued as to whether learning to read—a process that in some ways tends to enhance our sense of separation from the world—might somehow reinforce our sense of immersion in it.

The literacy unit was designed for specific places; however, the activities described could readily be used in other contexts. What these activities provide are examples of place-based initiatives that focus on imagination and ideas and strategies educators can use to develop their own place-focused units.

When I developed these examples, I was working as part of a research team that was designing an outdoor, place-based, imaginative education program in Maple Ridge, British Columbia.[17] This program was committed to fulfilling the standard mandated curriculum but it was also to be completely place-based and outside. There was no "classroom" to go into. With the exception of certain days when trips were taken indoors, different parks in Maple Ridge were to serve as the contexts for all learning. Typical pedagogical practice was thrown out the (non-existent) window. My role was to develop curriculum that would both support the aims of the school and employ cognitive tools that would maximize students' emotional and imaginative engagement.

Where Can IEE Be Implemented?

You might be wondering if it is possible to do IEE in an urban or suburban environment. Those of you living in locations with extreme climates—such as the Far North—might also be wondering what this approach would look like for your students. One premise of IEE is that we are surrounded by wildness—by which I mean that which we have not tamed— no matter where we are. The trick is to expand our own and our students' awareness so we can all experience this wildness in meaningful and memorable ways. This is what IEE can do. As students learn the mandated curriculum, IEE helps them understand how their bodies are engaged in the living world, regardless of the context (urban, suburban, or rural). Did you know that there is as much living diversity in one square metre of the soil surrounding a tree (even a tree planted in a city) as there is in an entire school? Students' discovery of the diversity of insect life around them—bugs, slugs, spiders, and worms— can occur in all contexts. With IEE as a guide, you can incorporate this diversity—this wildness—into a variety of curricular content.

Some of the activities I suggest for a temperate climate are obviously not possible in extreme climates where, for example, –20°C is common for many months of the year. Still, it is possible to bring the outdoors inside and to focus on the wonder of the natural environment—even the snow and ice—in all its beauty as well as its threats to our comfort and existence. Indeed, engaging with the wild forces of nature around us is part and parcel of extending our students' understanding of the world.

Wild/tame is one of the fundamental oppositions by which we make sense of our world. For our ancestors that opposition was also associated with danger/safety and fear/ security. Still today, knowing how to live with the duality of wild/tame is important for people who live in wilderness, including some First Nations people, country dwellers, and others who venture into wilderness. Our society's success in extending the areas of the tame, safe, and secure around us often leaves our children with little sense of what was for our ancestors a crucial daily concern—teaching their children the limits of the tamed world and the dangers of the wild. The beauty of the wild can be seen as tinged by a hidden and inevitable sense of its danger.

Introducing our students to the wild also represents an attempt to introduce them to a fundamental understanding of their world and their place in it. We cannot introduce them to the wild world, along with its associations with fear and danger, in the average school. So the challenge is to introduce the wild in a way that does not disguise the fact that wildness is not a naturally hospitable environment. While engaging students with the untamed features of our various environments, it is possible to show that our control of the wild world is partial and uncertain. So whatever the context—rural, suburban, or urban; temperate or extreme—there are dangers to be recognized in the realm of the wild. The conflict between the wild and the tame occurs in every context. Part of our job is to bring out that hidden conflict as we extend our students' understanding of the world.

What about Learning Outcomes?

You may be wondering what learning outcomes (also known as prescribed learning outcomes and intended learning outcomes) the weather and literacy units fulfill and also how these were used to shape the units. In IEE, learning outcomes are one part of a bigger concern for how to make knowledge meaningful to students. As teachers, we are concerned with much more than the learning outcomes. We are passionate about students' learning, about the topics we teach, and about having a beneficial impact on students' lives. We don't want to reduce student learning to a rigid set of outcomes, nor do we want to teach only to what we can assess or grade. So in this book, what guides my discussion is a concern with making knowledge meaningful and engaging students emotionally and imaginatively with their world as they learn the curriculum. This is a cognitive tools–based approach to learning, not an objectives-based one.

CHAPTER 3

STRATEGIES FOR ENGAGING STUDENTS' EMOTIONS IN LEARNING— A STUDY OF WEATHER

You will recall IEE's central claim: cultivation of ecological understanding requires emotional and imaginative engagement. That is, without emotional and imaginative engagement with knowledge, students' learning will not be memorable and its meaning will be superficial. This principle addresses the belief that students must feel something about the knowledge they are learning and the context in which they live if these are to become meaningful for them. Without feeling something about the diversity of life on the planet of which they are part and, in particular, about the places where they live, it is highly unlikely that students will come to develop a sense of concern or care for the earth.

IEE, unlike most current approaches designed to cultivate ecological understanding, centralizes emotional engagement in the planning process. It does so by shaping all teaching around those features of children's emotional and imaginative lives that engage them in the world. The term *kinds of understanding* refers to the way that human beings make sense of the world based on the kinds of learning tools they employ. For example, a young child employs the body's tools for making sense of the world. Some of the body's main learning tools include the five physical senses (smell, touch, hearing, sight, and taste), emotional responses, a sense of musicality, and a sense of incongruity. What results from employing the body's tools is a body-based or "somatic" understanding of the world.[1] IEE teachers can engage their students' emotions and imaginations by shaping topics in ways that employ these tools. (Somatic understanding is discussed in more detail in chapter 4.)

Human beings everywhere quickly develop oral language, after which a whole new set of learning tools becomes available for making sense of the world. These tools include the story form, vivid mental imagery evoked from words, a sense of mystery, binary opposites, and rhyme, rhythm, and pattern. Using such tools shapes a different kind of understanding of the world, one that Egan describes as a "mythic" understanding due, in part, to the similarities it has with features of cultures that are based on oral language.[2] A third kind of understanding develops as we become literate. Tools that accompany written language—including association with heroes, humanization of meaning, and a sense of wonder—shape what Egan calls a "romantic" understanding of the world.[3]

IEE recognizes, thus, the central role of language in learning. Our emotions and imaginations are engaged as we use and internalize the different learning tools afforded to us by language. Language is full of cultural inventions—learning tools—that help us to think and understand. In IEE, these learning tools—also called *cognitive tools*—are used to make content meaningful and memorable.

Cognitive Tools for the Primary and Elementary Grades

Table 2 provides an overview of some of the main tools that engage the imaginations of children in the primary and elementary grades. For children who are primarily oral language users and not yet reading fluently, these are vivid and powerful cognitive tools that can be used to tap into their imaginative lives.

TABLE 2. SOME TOOLS OF ORAL LANGUAGE—MYTHIC UNDERSTANDING

The story form	The story form is particularly powerful for imaginatively engaging with knowledge. Stories shape our emotional understanding of their content. Stories can shape real-world content as well as fictional material. It is the real-world story shaping that promises the most value for teaching.
Binary opposites	Binary opposites are a basic tool for organizing and categorizing knowledge. We see such opposites in conflict in nearly all stories, and they are crucial in providing an initial ordering to many complex forms of knowledge in the curriculum. Opposites such as security/fear, knowledge/ignorance, and competition/cooperation are emotionally charged and, when attached to curriculum content, imaginatively engaging.
Metaphor	Metaphor enables us to see one thing in terms of another. This peculiar ability lies at the heart of human intellectual inventiveness, creativity, and imagination. Helping students keep this ability vividly alive by exercising it frequently is important; using it often in teaching will help students learn with energy and flexibility.
Jokes and humour	Jokes and humour can expose some of the basic ways in which language works and, at the same time, allow students to play with elements of knowledge, thereby discovering some of learning's rewards. These tools can help to fight against rigid conventional use of rules; they encourage flexibility of mind.

TABLE 2. CONTINUED

Mental imagery evoked from words	Forming mental imagery from words can be of immense emotional importance, influencing us throughout our lives. In societies saturated by visual images, such as those of all Western and most Asian countries today, it is increasingly important to allow students to learn to generate their own mental images. Such images can carry more imaginative and memorable force than concepts alone. The use of mental images (as distinct from external pictures) should play a large role in all imaginative and ecological teaching.
Rhyme, rhythm, and pattern	Rhyme, rhythm, and pattern are tools for giving meaningful, memorable, and attractive shape to any content. Their roles in learning are numerous, and their power to engage the imagination in learning the rhythms and patterns of nature is enormous. They help us learn symbol systems and all the forms of knowledge and experience that we code into symbols.
Sense of mystery and puzzles	Recognition of mystery and puzzles develops an engagement with knowledge that is beyond students' everyday environment. It creates a sense of how much fascinating knowledge remains to be discovered. All subjects in the curriculum contain mysteries; part of our job in teaching any content is to point to the richer, deeper, and possibly unknown dimensions of knowledge. This can engage students' minds in the adventure of learning about the world around them.
Games, drama, and play	Games, drama, and play are often thought of as idle pleasures. Each, however, has an important role in learning. These tools represent some of the more basic forms of social interaction; they are easy to engage in and usually pleasurable. Each involves a series of skills, including the ability to fit events into a narrative, and can enlarge students' imaginative grasp of all knowledge in the curriculum.

The following sections provide practical examples of how the cognitive tools introduced in table 1 (see page 22) and table 2 can be used to shape a unit on weather for students in primary and elementary grades.

The Story Form and Binary Opposites

What's the story on weather? In other words, what is emotionally significant about it? What binary opposites shape the story of weather? In the following example, the binary opposites (the sources of dramatic tension) that are used to shape the content into a story form are hero versus villain and friend versus foe.

Human beings have a love-hate relationship with weather. We love it when it's "good" and we hate it when it's "bad"—and by this I mean bad enough to ruin plans for a family picnic as well as bad enough to evacuate coastal regions. Either way, we seem to constantly be talking about the weather. It could easily be the number one topic of conversation around the office water cooler. For good or bad, we depend on weather for life and are ultimately at its mercy for survival because it is centrally involved in the distribution and delivery of the basic conditions and requirements for life—water, sunlight, and air—that all living things rely on for survival. By controlling our basic life needs, weather can be personified as both hero and villain—it can give life and it can also take it away. If it gets cold enough, local fields become outdoor skating rinks. Weather is a friend. On the other hand, how often has it rained on sports day? Weather is a foe. These are examples that children can readily relate to. The main idea is that our story of weather as hero/friend also contains within it the story of weather as villain/foe. As students learn about weather, we want them to experience these emotionally engaging dimensions. Friend (rain for crops) becomes foe (flooding); hero (sunlight) becomes villain (drought, extreme heat, and skin cancer), and so on. If all goes well, students will finish their meteorological training with an acute sense of weather's role in life.

Metaphor

Terminology related to weather infuses our daily language: Lise has a sunny disposition; Peter, on the other hand, is often gloomy. How does each behave? You can bring this terminology to the attention of students throughout their meteorology study, for example, by exploring how weather is used metaphorically in language and discussing why this is the case. Why do we associate weather with human moods? Why is weather so often used to describe human traits and characteristics? Students can collect metaphors, expressions, and sayings related to weather and build a book of metaphors/analogies that link humans and atmospheric conditions.

You can ask younger students to explain an instance of weather terminology used in a sentence. For example, what does it mean when someone says: "My memory is a little foggy"? What mental image does this expression evoke? Can students draw this image? Older students could create sentences using weather terminology and explain what they mean. Students can also be encouraged to think about ways to explain how they are feeling using meteorological metaphors. Which type of atmospheric condition best describes their emotional state? Why, exactly, are they feeling "calm" or "stormy"? Who is feeling "under the weather"? What emotions does this involve?

Students might also investigate the origin of some weather-related expressions that are commonly used, for example: "It's raining cats and dogs!" What is the story here? My research into this expression has revealed numerous explanations, some more plausible than others. The most convincing account links the expression back to satirist Jonathan Swift and his vivid evocations of the unsanitary conditions of the streets of London in the seventeenth and eighteenth centuries. In a poem entitled "A Description of a City Shower," Swift reveals how a heavy rain could create a torrent of filthy water in the streets, a deluge that picked up off the streets, among other things, the carcasses of dead animals. The relevant lines from the poem read:

> Sweeping from butchers' stalls dung, guts, and blood;
> Drown'd puppies, stinking sprats, all drench'd in mud,
> Dead cats, and turnip-tops come tumbling down the flood.[4]

Could this be the origin of the expression we now use to explain a heavy rain? Those who think so argue that when Swift wrote in 1738, "I know Sir John will go, though he was sure it would rain cats and dogs,"[5] he was likely alluding to the image he had evoked in his earlier poem.

Jokes and Humour

You can suggest that students collect jokes about weather and then create their own jokes: Why did the woman go outside with her purse wide open? Because she was expecting some change in the weather! You can encourage students to enjoy the different kinds of weather they experience: How does it feel to cycle against a blustery wind? Isn't it funny when umbrellas blow inside out? You might have students imagine observing earth from afar. What would extraterrestrial beings think of people slipping and sliding around on icy ground? What kind of strange body covers do people wear when liquid falls from the sky? Are those smaller beings actually collecting what appears to be solid white material and rolling it into balls? Why? To throw them at each other? How odd!

Mental Imagery Evoked from Words

Evoking mental imagery from words can deepen students' understanding of different weather phenomena. For example, you might ask students to describe how they imagine "air." How do they describe the "nothing" of air that surrounds them? Is it nothing or is it something? You can instruct students to breathe in deeply, filling their lungs to maximum capacity and holding their breath. You might describe for students a canary-yellow balloon full to bursting with air. This balloon is so full that even a little more—the amount "exhaled" by a canary, perhaps—might cause it to explode. Now ask students to imagine the air escaping. Slowly, the taut latex balloon begins to relax, though still remaining tight. Encourage students to slowly release some of the air from their lungs. Continue to describe the balloon as it keeps releasing more air, its colour getting progressively darker as the tension releases. As students exhale the last of their breath, the balloon, too, shrivels as the last air escapes. It becomes limp, empty, but the students—hopefully!—breathe in again. Life goes on. You can now ask about the nature of the air: Is it something or is it nothing?

It might be helpful to draw students' attention to some traditional stories relating to air. In many Aboriginal cultures, the concept of awareness itself is closely connected to the air. In Navajo culture, for example, *nilch'i* is the concept used to describe the "Holy Wind." Abram describes how *nilch'i*, "meaning 'Wind, Air, or Atmosphere' suffuses all of nature, and is that which grants life, movement, speech, and awareness to all beings."[6] Students might look at their fingertips as they learn about how the Navajo explain the spiral patterns on them:

> Although invisible, the Holy Wind can be recognized by the swirling and spiraling traces it continually leaves in the visible world. The Winds that enter a human being leave their trace…in the vortices or swirling patterns to be seen on our fingertips and the tips of our toes, and in the spiraling pattern made by the hairs as they emerge from our heads.[7]

Students may never have thought much about the role of air in their lives. Have they considered, for example, that without internal wind—breath—we would not be able to speak, or even live? If we lose air, we lose life.

Greek and Roman myths, as well as local Aboriginal traditional stories, can be used to explore the meaning of different weather phenomena. For young children, you can read books aloud that evoke mental images of weather. For example, Karen Hesse's book *Come On, Rain!* vividly depicts the suffocating heat of summer before a sudden rainstorm brings the wilting and weary world back to life. Eric Carle's book *Little Cloud* can be used to encourage students to express some of the wonder, variety, and possibility that clouds offer the imagination.

Rhyme, Rhythm, and Pattern

As a child, I recall sitting in a circle and creating the sound of a rainstorm through light tapping, knee patting, clapping, hand rubbing, and so on. Students can play with the rhyme, rhythm, and pattern of spoken language to articulate their somatic experiences of various weather phenomena. Encourage them to focus on a form of weather with a distinctive sound pattern (e.g., rain, wind, or hail) and recreate the sound with their bodies. Then ask students to recreate the same sound with their voices, building on their somatic experience by playing with the sounds and patterns of oral language. They might work in small groups to recreate the sound of a rainstorm, windstorm, and so on. For young students, you might read aloud *Rain Drop Splash* by Alvin Tresselt, which embeds the sound of rain within a story of a raindrop's adventure.

Sense of Mystery and Puzzles

To engage a sense of mystery throughout the weather unit, you can pose questions that students will try to answer as they engage physically and emotionally with the weather. For example: "What happens to puddles after a rain? We saw them form, but where did they go?" Another example: Since the sun is in a different place in the sky early in the morning, at noon, and at the end of the school day, young students might think that the sun is moving around the earth—isn't this *obvious*? On a very sunny day, you can use shadows to show students how the sun and the earth move in relation to each other. Place a large object in an open space at the start of the school day. Have students trace the shadow on the ground and record the time. Repeat this two hours later. Continue keeping track of the time and the shape of the shadow of the object throughout the day. What happens? Why?

Games, Drama, and Play

Students can also learn about weather through structured and unstructured games, drama, and role play. They can be enlisted as "meteorologists in training," whose knowledge of the weather will come about through first-hand engagement that is largely unstructured. In other words, they will "play" with the weather they actually encounter and with the knowledge they are learning about weather. Freeze tag anyone? What about wind tag? (In wind tag, one or a few students are *it*. The rest of the class can be divided into different wind groups. So, for example, there might be some **gale-force winds**—these students run full out. There might be some **squalls**—these students can only run with short bursts of speed and for short periods of time. There might also be **breezes**—these students can only do slow jogging. **Tornado winds** must spin their way around the play area and have the special power to "free" the tagged students. Once freed, the tagged students also become tornado winds that spin until they, too, can pass on this wind power to someone else.) What about rain tag? Or weather charades? (In weather charades, groups or individual students can act out weather forecasts from the local radio station—for example: depictions of precipitation, winds, temperature, high and low pressure systems—so that other students can guess what weather is coming.)

Students can also role-play different weather patterns. For example, what characterizes an anticyclone or high-pressure front? How is the cyclone, or low-pressure front, different? Students can enact the turmoil that occurs when hot and cold fronts of air meet (this activity would likely involve lots of jumping and rolling). They can engage in dramatic representations of Ra (Egyptian god of the sun) meeting Zeus (Greek god of sky, lightning, and thunder) and, together, giving life to the world. Or they can be keepers (and representatives) of the north, south, east, and west winds. Students can read and enact some myths from ancient civilizations that describe the gods of the winds along with the ongoing conflicts and intrigues they engaged in. There are many ways students can play with weather topics; perhaps they could simply sing and dance in the rain or do some puddle jumping.

Cognitive Tools for the Middle and Secondary Grades

By middle or secondary school, you may use three different sets of cognitive tools to engage students: tools of the body, tools of oral language, and tools of literacy (see table 3). When we become literate, we lose some of the vividness that characterizes mythic understanding. And, similarly, when we develop a mythic understanding of the world, we lose some of the vividness of somatic understanding. In other words, with the gains that accompany the use of each set of tools, there are also losses. The aim of imaginative educators is to minimize the losses by continually engaging the many cognitive tools students have available to them.

TABLE 3. SOME TOOLS OF WRITTEN LANGUAGE—ROMANTIC UNDERSTANDING

Narrative structuring	This tool is related to our ability to best make sense of things when we can grasp their emotional meaning. A narrative context can evoke emotional significance as it conveys knowledge about, for example, physics or mathematics no less than about history or literature. Teaching in a narrative format involves asking about the content: "What's the story?"
Heroic qualities	Associating with heroes gives us the ability to imbue any aspect of reality with heightened importance. Being able to read and write greatly expands our consciousness and may result in a sense of concern as to where we fit into the world. By associating with a person, place, thing, or process that has heroic qualities or exceptional traits, literate students may overcome some of the feelings of alienation involved in a vast world whose limits are unknown. They can cling to a sort of safety net when the heroism of a person, place, thing, or process is revealed. They gain confidence that they, too, can face and deal with the real world as they imaginatively take on—and share in significant ways—the heroic qualities embedded in the topics of the curriculum.
Sense of wonder	A key tool in our initial explorations of reality is the sense of wonder. It enables us to focus on any aspect of the world around us, or the world within us, and see its particular uniqueness. It allows students to recognize something wonderful behind even the most routine and taken-for-granted things. The starting point of all inquiry is "I wonder why…?"
Humanizing meaning	This tool enables us to see beyond the surface of any knowledge to its source in human emotion. All knowledge is human knowledge, discovered or invented as a result of human emotions. This tool allows students to see knowledge through the emotions that were involved with its creation or current use, and so grasp its deeper human meaning.
Extremes of experience and limits of reality	When literate, we often engage imaginatively with the world by focusing on the extremes, the most exotic and bizarre features of reality, or the most terrible and courageous events. This kind of material is familiar from sensational newspapers and TV shows, and from publications such as *Guinness Book of World Records*. Focusing on extremes of experience and limits of reality powerfully engages students' imaginations in learning all curriculum content.

TABLE 3. CONTINUED

Collecting and organizing	Collections and hobbies provide another route for students to gain some security within the world they are learning about, even though they remain uncertain about its limits and dimensions. Gaining intellectual mastery of something gives assurance that the world is not limitless and can be understood in some significant degree. The normal profile for hobbies and collections is that they begin about the time an individual has begun to read and write, reach a peak of intensity around ages 11 to 13, and decline around age 15. In the imaginative classroom, teachers tap into this learning tool to make content more engaging. Every topic has within it some aspect students can collect or learn exhaustively.
The literate eye	The literate eye refers to opportunities that emerge when increased literacy allows reading and writing to play a larger role in organizing knowledge. Students can be imaginatively engaged in making and manipulating lists, flow charts, diagrams, and other documents.
Change of context and role play	The imagination can grasp the richer meaning of any context if we can view it from a different perspective. The change of context tool involves engaging differently with knowledge so that it isn't experienced like other topics in the curriculum. By shifting the context in which knowledge is learned—by, for example, enlisting students to take on a different role or by metaphorically transforming the classroom into another place, time or circumstance, or even by you, the teacher, becoming a different person—students' imaginations can be brought vividly to life, engaging the material much more richly.

The rest of this chapter addresses cognitive tools that can be used to shape a unit on weather for students in middle and secondary grades. The tools are not always employed individually, but are often employed in combination. The tools of "a sense of wonder," as well as of "change of context and role play," are infused throughout the activities. The tool of "the literate eye" is connected to the tool of "collecting and organizing."

We begin with a different kind of story-structuring than the example provided earlier in this chapter for young children. Now the topic of weather is shaped in a way that evokes a heroic quality, tapping into this particular feature of the literate student's imaginative life.

Narrative Structuring and Heroic Qualities

What's the story on weather? What heroic quality can shape the story of weather and leave students feeling emotionally engaged? How do *you* engage with different aspects of the weather? One transcendent quality that points to the emotional significance of weather—and that can make the topic more meaningful for students—is that it is life-giving. This can be the core of a heroic narrative about weather.

Our understanding of weather as a life-giving force depends on many factors including, for example, where and when we live. For some people who live, work, and play indoors most of the time, the weather may only have a marginal impact on their lives. The daily probability of precipitation may influence decisions about wardrobe (what should I wear today?), forms of transportation (should I walk or is it going to rain? Do I need an umbrella?), and exercise or entertainment (should I run trails, go to the gym, or maybe just stay on the sofa?). If you live in a mild climate, the daily aspects of weather may not be a major factor in your life even if you work or play outdoors. If you live in a harsh climate, where the daily atmospheric conditions can include extremes of all kinds, the impact of the weather is much greater and awareness of its life-giving aspects becomes much stronger. If you live in a tornado zone, for example, wind patterns can obviously be tied to life and death.

If we look back to pre-industrial times or to societies (current or historical) whose interdependence with the natural world forms a central part of their consciousness and culture, we find that people are much more acutely aware of the life-giving quality of weather. Their understanding of the implications of weather is also more somatic and place-based. Our lifestyles may have changed, but the life-giving nature of weather has not. For example, atmospheric conditions—temperature, wind, clouds, and precipitation—influence how well crops grow. Today, we have advanced technologies to extend the growing period for crops and bioengineered species that can withstand variations in weather, but we cannot grow crops if there is inadequate sunshine, rain, and temperature.

Humanizing Meaning

To engage students' interest in the human dimension of what they are learning, you can present stories about people who are committed to working with weather, learning about it, or even risking their lives during severe weather. To what extremes will people go to learn about the weather? Is the pursuit of weather knowledge for work or pleasure? Consider storm chasing. This activity is defined as "the pursuit of any severe weather condition, regardless of motive, which can be for curiosity, adventure, scientific exploration, or for news or media coverage."[8] Someone who chases storms is known as a "storm chaser, or simply a chaser."[9] While serious chasers frequently follow tornadoes, many also chase thunderstorms and hurricanes.

If putting oneself at risk to learn about the weather makes one a "chaser," Benjamin Franklin qualified. In 1752 he climbed atop a church during a thunder and lightning storm to conduct his infamous kite and key experiment that showed the connection between lightning and electricity. (Don't try this at home!) David Hoadley is widely considered the pioneer storm chaser. He began chasing North Dakota storms in 1956 and founded *Stormtrack* magazine. Meteorologist Neil Ward was the first scientific storm chaser. He developed ideas about thunderstorm and tornado structure and evolution, as well as forecasting techniques.

To engage the human dimensions of weather, you can also elaborate on the metaphorical dimensions of weather. For example, students can think about what weather best describes a grumpy uncle, a big (or little) sister, a favourite music star, and so on. Who is their most loved person? What kind of weather best represents this person? What kind of weather do students associate with themselves?

Extremes of Experience and Limits of Reality

There are countless extremes and limits about weather that students can learn about. For example, on a really windy day students can imagine how much *more* windy it is in a hurricane or tornado. You can encourage students to identify their own "record-breakers" throughout the year, for example: the hottest and coldest days, most consecutive days of rain, most amount of rainfall, or largest accumulation of snow or hail. Students can also research and compile information on record-breaking aspects of weather farther afield, for example: the most destructive storms, longest droughts, biggest deluge, record high and low temperatures. Where and when did these occur?

Why do some parts of the world have very harsh weather conditions? Why do some places, such as the central United States and Australia, experience frequent tornadoes? There are 500 to 600 tornadoes in the US each year. Is there any record of a tornado near where your students live? What is the origin of a tornado? That is a question that even top scientists cannot answer definitively.

Collecting and Organizing: Learning about Precipitation, Sunshine and Temperature, and Wind and Air

Two powerful tools that engage the literate mind are collecting and organizing. A fascination with collecting things tends to coincide with literacy. Between the ages of 7 and 13, children around the world collect things such as hockey cards, shells, stickers, stamps, and coins. It may be that collecting something gives us a sense of confidence, a sense that within the vast world we have a comprehensive understanding of some small piece of it. With literacy, we also begin to access more information through the eye, and we often enjoy ordering, reordering, classifying, and categorizing that information. Playing with information visually pleases the literate mind. The following examples explore how these two cognitive tools—collecting and organizing (the literate eye)—can be employed in relation to units on Precipitation (labelled (P)); Sunshine and Temperature (labelled (S)); and Wind and Air (labelled (W)).

Collecting: Distinguishing forms of precipitation (P)

Most students have direct experience with a variety of forms of precipitation. As part of their meteorological training, they will learn to distinguish between different kinds of precipitation, enriching their vocabulary in the process. Yes, it's wet, but what kind of rain is this? Yes, it's cold—is that sleet?

The following are some common types of precipitation:

- **Drizzle** (a liquid)
- **Freezing drizzle** (a liquid that freezes on impact, creating sheets of ice on roads and other surfaces)
- **Rain** (a liquid)
- **Sleet** (a solid "freezing rain" or rain/snow mix that includes ice pellets)
- **Snow** (a solid)
- **Graupel** (a solid "soft" hail including snow pellets)
- **Hail** (a solid composed of lumps of ice between 5–150 mm in size; usually in thunder clouds (cumulonimbi)

Did you know that the biggest hailstone ever recorded was the size of a soccer ball? This car-denter (skull-cracker!) was over 17.8 cm (7 inches) in diameter and fell in Nebraska in June 2003. Students might be interested in learning about some bizarre forms of precipitation that we don't often hear about and may never actually experience on the ground. These include the following:

- **Virga** (precipitation that evaporates before hitting the surface of the earth)
- **Diamond dust** (hexagonal-shaped ice needles/crystals that fall at approximately −40°C)
- **Thundersnow** (solid precipitation that falls in rare conditions of winter thunderstorms or thunder snowstorms)

To help students gather more information about precipitation, they can keep track of days of rainfall (for future seasonal comparisons), quantity of rain, rates of absorption, or the appearance of the rain. Using microscopes, students can also look closely at water droplets and then draw and label what they see.

Collecting: Recording changes (P)

For this activity, each student can focus on a small area, making close observations of how precipitation leads to short- and long-term change. What impact does precipitation have on a place? What do animals and insects do in rain? How do they adapt to different forms of precipitation? How does rain physically change the colours of a place?

Collecting: Observing the water cycle (P)

Observing changes that occur in a place during and after a rainstorm can provide a natural entry point into discussions about the water cycle. Students may be amazed to learn that there is no more water on the planet now than there was billions of years ago.

The water cycle is a story of recycling at its best. You can evoke a mental image so that students get a sense of the forces at play. For example, during evaporation, moisture is sucked from the ground into the air but during precipitation, moisture is pulled down towards the earth due to a combination of atmospheric pressure and gravity.

Collecting: Catching clouds (P)

During this unit on weather, some students may choose to collect clouds. They can spend time observing the sky and sketching the shapes they see in their journals. In this "collecting" stage of the unit, students can deepen their understanding of clouds and should be encouraged to not only document shape but also other characteristics of clouds including, for example, their apparent thickness, approximate location, colour, and movement. Students can track the connection between certain kinds of clouds and precipitation. Based on students' observations of the kinds of clouds that release precipitation, what do they forecast? Cloud catching will also provide an opportunity for students to consider the scientific names of different kinds of clouds and the characteristics of the troposphere.

Collecting: Mapping impacts (P)

To support students in understanding the impact of weather where they live, you can encourage them to collect visual representations of how rain affects different areas. For example, students can map how precipitation shapes the local ecology. Which areas are the wettest? Which stay the driest? Students can hypothesize why the amount of precipitation affects the local ecology in various ways.

Collecting: Noticing patterns of rainfall (P)

Students can deepen their understanding of precipitation and patterns of rainfall if they measure the amount of rainfall in a week, month, or season. You can first invite students to design a means of collecting rain, either by using natural objects or some basic supplies. Students might imagine that they are trapped without water. If they don't collect the most amount of rainwater, they will not survive. Which group can collect the most? Students can measure how much they collect, noting the impact of different kinds of rain on quantity.

Organizing: Expressing learning about precipitation (P)

The objective for this part of the unit is for students to shape the information they have collected—both objective information and their subjective experiences—in a way that demonstrates what they have learned about weather. Depending on the age of the students, you can provide guidelines for organizing the information or leave the classification up to the students.

Always encourage students to be imaginative in their expressions of learning. For example, they may use digital images, sketches, or written or verbal descriptions to document the changes that they have observed in their chosen places. Students can be encouraged to think about how colour, noise, and/or sound could be used to represent the weather of their local place. They may opt to express their understanding through a documentary presentation, musical performance, or by using a personal diary to track their meteorological training. Using their imaginations, students can also take on totally different perspectives: How might a tree express its understanding of the weather? How might a local stream or river understand or experience different weather phenomena?

Organizing: Using tables, charts, and graphs (P)

Students can organize and analyze the information they have collected and use it to create graphs indicating amounts of rainfall, wettest months per year, or wettest days/weeks per month. Students can graph the quantity of rainfall, comparing the quantity to the kinds of precipitation (refer back to page 40). They could create visual organizers to represent kinds of clouds.

Collecting: Appreciating the gifts of sunlight (S)

As with the precipitation-focused learning activities, collecting data is a more imaginatively engaging and place-based activity if students make their observations in particular spots that they choose in their immediate environments. Encourage students to select a specific place to focus their investigations of sunshine and temperature.

In this activity, you can begin by asking students to consider what sunlight does for us. What are its gifts? What evidence or examples of these gifts can students find? They may use their journals to record examples of the life-giving nature of sunlight by tracking the growth of a plant. They may use photography to capture the colour changes in the world that occur on a sunny day. Alternatively, they may collect shadows. They can be challenged to find the hints of shadows on a cloudy day. Shade, too, is a gift. What are the gifts of particularly hot days? (Swimming in a lake? Outdoor picnics? Sleeping under the stars?) What are the gifts of particularly cold days?

Collecting: Tracking temperature (S)

Students can keep track of temperatures daily and seasonally, and then begin to describe the changes in temperature in more specific ways. At what temperature do they consider it hot? Warm? Cool? What words, colours, or images can students use to describe various temperatures? One aim of having students keep records of temperature variations daily and seasonally is that they can then use this information to draw conclusions about temperature patterns.

You can encourage students to collect extremes in temperature. Will it get so hot in June that we can fry an egg on the sidewalk or bake cookies in a locked car? How quickly does an ice cube melt? How quickly does water evaporate? Where does it get the hottest on a summer day? How hot can it get in this place? Why is it so hot there? Where does it remain coolest? Why is this so? Why do black objects get burning hot while white objects tend not to? These are all "wonder" questions that students can investigate. They can design and conduct the experiments leading to answers.

Organizing: Finding the story (S)

Students might organize the information they have been collecting about temperature and sunshine in a story form or narrative. What is emotionally engaging—interesting, wonderful, intriguing—about sunshine, heat, warmth? What happens to this place as the sun comes out and the temperature rises or falls? As "reporters" for a news broadcast, students could describe their places in ways that engage their listeners and evoke the emotional significance of the topic that they have identified.

Organizing: Using tables, charts, and graphs (S)

How might students make their weather knowledge readily available to others? They can use a bar graph to indicate high and low temperatures per month. At the end of the school year, they can use a circle graph to show the percentage of cloudy versus sunny days. They might compare their temperature data with the positions of the sun, which they may also have recorded. What is the relationship between the position of the sun and the temperature?

Collecting: Observing wind speed, direction, and impact (W)

As in the earlier collecting activities, students can collect and organize information about many aspects of wind and air. For this activity, divide students into wind teams. Each team will need to decide on a wind-related name and create a flag that will represent their team. The students will use their flags to indicate different wind directions and keep track of where the wind comes from over a period of time. As a team, they will decide how to measure wind speed. You can encourage students to decide on ways to determine low, moderate, and high wind speeds (for example, by the wind's impact on any structures they build or the dispersal of material). Students can observe and record the impact of wind on the natural world. What evidence of wind is found in the forest? How do animals and plants respond to wind?

Collecting: Classifying winds (W)

Meteorologists classify different kinds of winds based on speed, strength, and duration. Students can add the following classifications to their ongoing weather collections and lists of meteorological vocabulary:

- **Gusts** (short bursts of wind; various wind speeds)
- **Squalls** (strong winds of intermediate duration—approximately one minute)
- **Breeze, gale, storm, hurricane, tornado, or typhoon** (winds of long duration— for example, thunderstorm flows lasting more than ten minutes and breezes lasting a few hours—with speeds ranging from low to high)
- **Dust devils** (small whirlwinds or tornadoes)

What gesture best represents each type of wind? Encourage students to brainstorm words that best describe each wind's "personality" by asking some questions: Would you rather sit next to someone on the bus who has a stormy personality or someone who is gusty? Would you rather your next math test be a breeze or a typhoon? How, exactly, would you run if you were a breeze? A gale? A gust? Students could experiment by running and changing their speed, directionality, and stride to indicate different types of wind.

Collecting: Studying how wind shapes the earth (W)

One reason that winds are central to mythology is that they are so powerful. What evidence can students find of the long-term impacts of wind? Wind plays a major role in shaping the earth's surface by eroding, transporting, and depositing material. Wind also plays a role in fertilization of plants. How and where does this occur?

Collecting: Creating wind activities (W)

Suggest that students use what they have learned about wind and its impact on the earth to create an activity or game. For example, divide students into small groups and give each group one aspect of the weather unit to shape into an activity for their peers to enjoy. Their challenge is to deepen their peers' understanding of a wind type through movement or gesture. No words are allowed. How might one use movement to differentiate between a gust and a squall? How does the north wind blow?

Collecting: Finding the music of wind (W)

Suggest that students listen for the "music" that emerges from the sway of branches on a windy day. Encourage them to identify different patterns of sound and to apply various features of musicality to the sounds (for example: qualities of tone, tempo, volume, and rhythm). How might they classify the sounds? What different tones can they hear? How long do the sounds last? What features of the sounds dominate? In what ways could students recreate these sounds? Can they incorporate this music into a song of celebration of the air?

Ongoing Activities

The following activities are immediately useful for older students but can also be easily adapted for younger students. The aim is to give students more creative freedom than other activities offer. Multiple cognitive tools are combined in these ongoing activities, such as narrative understanding (the story form), the sense of wonder, the sense of mystery, mental imagery evoked from words, identification of heroic qualities, collecting and organizing, the literate eye, and humanizing meaning.

Diary of a Weather Watcher

Provide students with the opportunity to keep a weather journal during unstructured writing/sketching time. Encourage them to describe as vividly as possible what they experience somatically—smells, textures, sights, sounds, and tastes. (Hopefully, a sky described as "blue" will, with time, become azure, eggshell blue, or crushed amethyst!) Are students demonstrating any emotional response or reaction to various weather conditions? What are their reactions? How are they "weathering the weather"? How do other-than-human inhabitants (animals, insects, and birds) deal with the weather? The goal of a weather diary is for students to have a medium for expressing both what they experience and how they feel about the weather phenomena they experience. To develop their journals, they can have unstructured writing and drawing opportunities but they can also be guided with prompts that stem from unit activities. The text that follows is taken from my weather diary.

Diary of a Weather Watcher

Monday, April 4—Seriously! Why does it seem to rain so much on Mondays? This morning the rain was a relentless mist. Now the drops are more distinct, heavier, puddle-making. Still no wind. I feel damp.

Monday, April 11—Too cold today to take my writing outside. But it is tempting—for the first time in days the world seems awake under the rays of the sun. I'm alerted to an odd combination of atmospheric play. Out a window to my right, I see a crystal blue sky, streaked with greyish, thin clouds. A breeze moves amongst the branches of a leafless tree. But the sound of a heavy, increasingly loud drumming sound calls my attention behind me. Out the window behind me, the sky is black, and heavy rain mixed with sleet falls. Still no rain from the window to my right, and yet behind me the rain is so thick I can't make out the trees. Among the raindrops that strike the ground, hail bounces to varying heights. I think of the kids at the local school, clocking in their running club circuits, undoubtedly soaked. I think, too, of my garden and of the refreshing rain that enriches the soil, preparing it for upcoming planting. Five minutes have passed, and so has the rain. Sun shines through windows streaked with new rain (but rain is never really "new"). I'm now outside. Following this sudden "dump" of water, the world smells different. It smells wet. It smells clean—the air has just been "showered by the shower." Wet earth is now pocked with the impact of the hailstones that still lay scattered among rocks and leaves. The grass emits a deep, earthy smell. This—for me, for now—is what "wet" smells like.

Monday, May 2—I think the last few days of warmer weather have led the tree outside my window into believing it is spring. Or so it seems as I stare up through its branches. There are buds emerging that were not on the tree's branches last week. The tree branches move only slightly in a breeze, almost unnoticeable if the hairs tickling my face didn't alert me to this particular atmospheric condition. The tree's branches stand out like silhouettes against an overcast sky. Sunshine is forecast for later today.

Wednesday, May 18—There's a different feeling in the air today. For one, my body is met by a warmth it hasn't felt much lately. The flowers, like the birds that call out in song, seem to be yearning for this warmth to last. A thin layer of clouds makes an otherwise deep blue sky hazy. From time to time, a breeze blows; blades of grass tickle my toes and the hair on my arms brings my alertness to my body.

Collecting Weather Data

You may have students design a chart or table where they can keep track of the weather conditions as a class, day by day, including duration of sunlight, daily temperature (high/low), wind speed, wind direction, description of precipitation, amount of precipitation, and so on. This can be an ongoing class project that differs from students' individual weather "collections." Students may use symbols or text to describe weather conditions. As they progress through the weather unit, they can refine, revise, and adapt the table to capture more nuanced aspects of weather. They can use this data for graphing or measurement activities in mathematics or science. Students may use digital cameras to photograph changes and, by dating the photographs, may be able to describe more accurately the seasonal changes they observe. They may put the data they collect to music or represent it in other pictorial/graphic forms.

The Mystery of Air

A study of weather shouldn't omit the sensuous medium in which it all takes place—the air. Abram describes the air as a great enigma for the human senses; it is simultaneously inescapably present and also alarmingly absent.[10] At times, we are alert to the air's presence all around us as its movement tickles the hairs on our arms or sweeps papers off our desks. Its temperature causes our flesh to retract and its smell evokes a vivid mental image of another place or time. We rely on air to fill our lungs and provide the oxygen our blood needs in order for us to survive. At the same time, however, air constantly escapes our vision—the sense of sight upon which we so often rely to prove what is real. What we see are the effects of air on features of the world around us, as Abram describes:

> I can see the steady movement it induces in the shape-shifting clouds, the way it bends the branches of the cottonwoods, and sends ripples along the surface of the stream. The fluttering wing features of a condor soaring overhead; the spiraling trajectory of a leaf as it falls; a spider web billowing like a sail; the slow drift of a seed through space—all make evident, to my eyes, the sensuous presence of the air. Yet these eyes cannot see the air itself.[11]

Throughout their meteorological training, you can engage students in the mystery of air by having them look for clues of invisible air. Like detectives, students might keep track of these clues in their weather journals, hoping to collect enough evidence to prove the existence of the "nothing" air around them. What evidence is there if we can't see it directly? How are human beings like fish? They are immersed, like fish, in a substance that gives them life.

In Western culture, the air has little significance beyond our scientific understanding of its role in life. This is not the case in most Aboriginal cultures in North America; the air is sacred.[12] Abram describes how different Aboriginal cultures associate wind/air/breath with the creation of the world, life, and awareness. For the Lakota nation, for example, the most sacred spirit is the "Enveloping Sky." It is "felt to be everywhere, the omnipresent spirit that imparts life, motion, and thought to all things, yet is visible to us only as the blue of the sky."[13] You might ask students what the air means to them. Why do we tend to forget about air? How might we honour it? Is it worth honouring? Chapter 4 includes some suggestions for introducing the significance of air through story and imagery.

Weather Reports and Forecasts

As part of a morning routine, students may take turns providing a weather report of current atmospheric conditions and a forecast. For the forecast, they could make an educated guess based on their observations of the conditions they experience in the morning or they could propose really extreme conditions (for example: hailstones the size of soccer balls in May or record-breaking high temperatures in December). Other students in the class can predict whether the student meteorologist's daily forecast will be accurate or not. Partners or teams can be awarded points for accurate predictions and students can be awarded points for correctly determining if the student meteorologists were right or wrong. You might also have students note how frequently the weather can be similar to the previous day's weather. Is there more change or more stability from day to day? If stability is common, does this mean that the most accurate forecast is: "Tomorrow's weather will be like today's"? Or does the weather more often change from day to day? What is the basis for official forecasts? How reliable are these forecasts?

Conclusion

The "feeling" principle is all about connecting students emotionally and imaginatively with what they are learning. By using the tools described in this chapter, it is possible for students to *feel* something about weather because their knowledge is tied up with facets of their imaginative lives. As a result, knowledge becomes meaningful and memorable.

CHAPTER 4

STRATEGIES FOR ENGAGING THE BODY IN LEARNING—A STUDY OF WEATHER

Imagine a baby boy. Wide-eyed, he meets the world around him. All ears, he hears the varied sounds in his immediate environment, soothed by the familiar and also startled—or pleasantly surprised—by the unexpected. With his eyes, ears, hands, mouth, and nose, he learns about the world through what he can see, hear, touch, taste, and smell. The world is a wonder of textures, temperatures, and tones. The stimuli he senses evoke emotional responses—he makes initial meaning of his context. He is inseparable from it. He is immersed. Play with a baby and see the joy experienced by sensory engagement with patterns of sound and texture—crackles, pops, pings, bangs, and bongs never cease to amuse. Smile and coo and you will likely get a smile back; the baby's smile is an indication of his need for support within networks of love and care.

The activeness principle[1] aims to nurture this kind of understanding of the world: a somatic, or body-based, one. The challenge faced by educators interested in developing students' sense of the body's engagement in the world and the body's understanding of knowledge is that, as language users, they are less able to experience the world with their bodies than babies can. The human body's tools for understanding lose some of their power as we employ the tools of oral language and then the increasingly complex tools of written language. If only my mother had told me when I began to babble that this milestone in my development also marked the end of an era! I can never go back to a purely somatic understanding of the world because, from the point I began to babble, I would forever after employ the tools of language to mediate my understanding of the world.

Although IEE educators acknowledge that with the gains of language also come losses, the aim is to nurture the body's learning tools in order to maximize the gains and minimize the losses. Table 4 outlines some of the powerful tools that teachers can use to make learning more meaningful by engaging their students' imaginations and bodies with the content of the curriculum. Students at all levels of schooling possess these somatic tools to greater or lesser extents.

TABLE 4. SOMATIC UNDERSTANDING—SOME OF THE BODY'S LEARNING TOOLS

The senses	The senses are the body's tools of observation through which we understand the world in detail. Their pedagogical importance is linked to their role in stimulating emotions and imagination. Emotions and imagination are immediately engaged by what is directly encountered through the body's senses. In other words, what we see, hear, smell, touch, and taste means something to us because of our emotions. In teaching IEE, educators focus on both the senses and the emotional responses they evoke.
Emotional response	Emotional response is one of the most basic ways in which human beings make sense of their experiences. It orients us towards knowledge or experience. When something is meaningful to us—when it makes sense—the meaning is tied up with a human emotion. Emotions are important sense-making tools for all kinds of understanding, not solely that associated with the body.
Gesture	Human beings frequently communicate meaning with the body. We are born with the ability to use actions, or gestures, to convey meaning and also to understand the meaning or intention of other people's gestures. While our gestures can convey meaning on their own, we often employ them to reinforce what we are trying to convey through oral language. Gesture ties up knowledge with emotional responses and a body-based understanding and helps us to learn.
Sense of incongruity and humour	The sense of humour emerges soon after we are born. It is often sparked by recognition of incongruity: the intentional or unintentional interruption of a pattern is a source of pleasure. The recognition of incongruity is also a learning tool. Egan identifies the body's sense of humour/incongruity as a possible source of the flexibility of thought that can ultimately lead to a sense of irony.[2] Moreover, the smiles and laughs that accompany this tool also function to help us form relationships and participate in networks of care.
Sense of pattern and musicality	Human beings are innately musical. By this I mean that we possess the ability to recognize pattern in the world around us. In our youngest years, through identification of significant patterns of sound, sight, touch, taste, and smell, we gain an initial understanding of how the world is organized. We identify patterns both through our senses and in movements such as walking, running, or dancing.[3] These patterns or rhythms are a source of aesthetic delight. Our ability to recognize pattern also enables us to understand and use complex symbol systems (e.g., in mathematics or language).

The following activities are divided into two groups—not because they should be considered completely separate but, rather, because they might be used to build upon one another.

The first set, "Engaging the Body with the Weather," provides students with opportunities for learning about weather phenomena by engaging the body's tools. Most of the activities draw on a combination of tools. For example, one activity might focus on the senses as well as emotional responses.

The second set, "Honouring," suggests ways students can demonstrate what they have learned, build upon their somatic experiences, and celebrate their awareness of their involvement in the world around them.

Engaging the Body with the Weather

The following activities provide students with opportunities for learning about weather phenomena through use of the body's tools as described in table 4. While it is not essential to conduct these activities outdoors, you are encouraged to do so whenever possible. The overarching *story* of the life-giving nature of weather and the dramatic play of friend/foe can be most powerfully experienced by students outside classroom walls.

Doing Yoga: Engaging the Senses and Evoking Emotional Responses

Some of you might ask: "What does yoga have to do with learning? Are we wasting valuable pedagogical time with yoga?" If IEE teachers aim to enhance students' awareness of their bodies and their ability to engage imaginatively with the world around them using the body's tools, yoga is a valuable approach. Practising some basic yoga postures helps students become aware of their bodies and engages mental imagery, both of which can deepen students' understanding of the topics they are learning about. If possible, take students outside to do these poses.

Stillness is educationally valuable. It affords students the opportunity to enter into an immersive relationship with the natural world. This is one aspect of *activeness* that an imaginative and ecological educational approach aims to support. You will recall that the activeness principle is not about "being active"; instead, it refers to immersive types of encounters with the world. Physical movement may be a part of activeness, but activeness is often achieved through lingering or pausing. Or, as in the yoga practice suggested here, through stillness.

Tadasana (The Mountain)

Tadasana is the mountain pose (*tada* means "mountain"):

> [T]he body is as steady and as still as a mountain. The weight is evenly distributed on the feet and the arms are at the sides. The spine is lengthened and the back of the neck straight.[4]

Begin by encouraging students to focus on their breathing and what it means to be a mountain—stillness, strength, immensity, majesty. Guide students towards a stillness and mindfulness that they may not be accustomed to. As they stand still and strong, ask them to focus their senses on the air around/on them. How do they feel it? How do they hear it? See it? Smell it? Taste it? If students are doing this pose outside on a rainy or snowy day, ask them how they experience the precipitation. Is the rain hitting them in distinctive drops? Are flakes of snow settling on their shoulders? Tickling their noses? Or is the rain or snow encompassing them in a kind of blanket?

Shavasana (The Corpse)

Shavasana is the corpse or dead-body pose (*shava* means "corpse"). *Shavasana* in particular can draw students' attention to their breath:

> [T]he body lies on the floor face-up and completely relaxed, while the mind is alert. The eyes are closed, the arms at the sides with the palms up. The body remains as motionless as a corpse.[5]

In *shavasana,* students are encouraged to stay as still as possible. The challenge is to resist all movement—they should try not to itch, scratch, wipe, or even blink their eyes. They should try to find the stillness of a dead body. Of course, unlike a corpse, they have breath and can focus their attention on breathing. Help students to focus on their breath through guided breathing: deep, slow inhalations and long, slow exhalations. Encourage students to bring their alertness to their bodies, experiencing their engagement with the air around their bodies.

The corpse pose is particularly good for drawing students' attention to clouds. In stillness, focusing on their breathing, students can gaze up at the clouds. They can observe their shape or watch them change shape as they move across the sky.

Padmasana (The Lotus)

Padmasana is the lotus pose, done sitting on the floor or ground:

> [T]he legs are crossed... the spine is erect, the hands either placed on the knees, palms up, or resting in the lap.[6]

Children, because they are flexible, might find it easy to get into a crossed-ankles position. Staying still in the position requires a lot of practice, however; many students need to practise stillness and mental calmness.

In lotus posture, students can be encouraged to centre themselves, to be mindful of how they are experiencing the sunshine and/or the temperature. What do their foreheads feel like? What emotions are evoked?

Bhujangasana (The Cobra)

Bhujangasana is the serpent or cobra pose:

> [It] starts from a downward-facing position with the palms of the hands flat on the floor below the shoulders. The spine is lengthened and the buttocks firmed as the head and chest are slowly lifted. The elbows stay close to the body and the eyes look up. The return to the original position is made slowly.[7]

As part of a study of wind, you can focus on yoga breathing to engage students somatically in feeling the presence of air in this posture. First draw their attention to the shared nature of air. Have students ever stopped to consider that plants breathe too? (Breathing can be a metaphor for photosynthesis.) Have students stopped to consider that they are only one species in a world of breathing entities that rely on the air for existence?

Urikshasana (The Tree)

Urikshasana is the tree pose:

> [A] steady, rooted stance is created by bringing one foot against the inner thigh of the other, standing, leg. The knee of the raised leg is out to the side and the pelvis opened. The arms are raised from the namaste position at the chest and are stretched up over the head, just as the limbs of a tree lift to the sunlight. The pose is repeated on the opposite side.[8]

You can ask students to imagine being something other than themselves to try to bring into focus what wind feels like. For example, students may feel the air/wind as though they were trees. Encouraging students to pause and think about the qualities that a tree represents may begin to evoke a deeper understanding than only the obvious physical features of a tree. Doing this pose may lead into a discussion of qualities that include uprightness, rootedness, strength, and alignment.

As students practise this posture, guide and encourage them to breathe deeply and ask them to be mindful of their bodies. How, like a tree, do they feel the wind? How do they interact with the wind without losing their balance? Are they firmly rooted? Do they feel strong or vulnerable in the pose? The book *Hatha Yoga: The Hidden Language* suggests additional questions that may arise for students as they practise the tree pose:

> Where have my roots spread? Where do they get their nourishment? Which are mine and which belong to someone else? What competes with my roots for nourishment?[9]

Many teachers do not focus on the body's engagement in their practice, let alone give students time to linger in ways described above. By engaging in some yoga practice, along with other tools to be discussed, students can learn course content in ways that bring into focus their personal engagement in a living world of wonder. They will begin to develop a sense of being embedded in the world and, simultaneously, an increasing familiarity with the places in which they live.

Listening to the Rain: Engaging the Sense of Pattern and Musicality

Different kinds of rain create very different sounds. Consider, for example, the sound of drizzle or mist versus a downpour. Imaginative educators can encourage students to focus on the sound patterns of rain. What's the loudest rain? The quietest? The quickest? The slowest? Students can work in small groups to recreate the sounds of rain by using their bodies to drum, clap, stamp, and so on. They may use their voices—as well as natural objects they find around them—to create different sounds and perhaps record them to replay at a later time.

Looking at the Rain: Engaging the Sense of Pattern and Musicality

Different kinds of rain wet the world—and our bodies—differently. What visual patterns do students notice in the way the ground gets wet? What patterns do they notice in the way their clothes, skin, or hair gets wet? What areas get wet the fastest? The slowest? In what places does nature provide shelter? Where are nature's "umbrellas" open? Students can draw the different patterns they notice and map the best natural places to stay dry in the rain.

Smelling the Rain: Engaging the Senses

Does rain have a smell? What does it mean when we say, "It smells like rain"? Do different kinds of rain have different kinds of smells? How does a place smell before versus after some rain? Which smell do students prefer? What words describe the smell of rain?

Feeling the Heat, Feeling the Cold: Engaging the Senses

How can students determine with their bodies a rise in temperature? How do their bodies respond to heat? How do their bodies respond to cold? What gets really *hot* on a summer day? How do objects feel, smell, and look different in the morning, at the start of the school day, compared to later in the day, in full sun?

Feeling the Weather: Evoking Emotional Responses

Different kinds of weather can evoke or contribute to different states of mind. Encourage students to keep track of their emotions on various days: Do they notice a relationship between their moods and the weather? Do they *feel* differently on sunny days compared to cloudy or rainy days? How might students complete this sentence: "Sunshine makes me feel…"? Ask students to consider how the world actually looks different on a sunny day.

Do they notice anything different about the colours around them? Do they notice more activity? In addition to humans, what other creatures come out on a sunny day? How do shadows affect the appearance of their surroundings?

Breathing the Air: Engaging the Senses

Abram describes the air as "the felt matrix of our breath and the breath of the other animals and plants and soils."[10] He laments that we are mostly unaware of the air around us because we can't directly *see* it. Indeed, it is through engaging our senses of smell, touch, taste, and hearing that we can experience the air.

To engage students emotionally and imaginatively with the air, you can focus on the richness of the air in the way Abram suggests. That is, the imagination can be engaged by alerting students to the multiple influences and constituents of the air.

You can encourage students to imagine the air not as an empty void but a collective medium of breath—a medium that human beings literally share with the living world around them as they breathe in and out. You can help students to be mindful of how their lives inseparably connect, through their breath, with humans and other living things around them. Students can become mindful of the role plants play in cleaning the air.

You can encourage students to describe the subtleties of smell that they notice in their local contexts. How is the air different—in smell, but also perhaps in texture—in different locations? Can students articulate what is unique about different smells? Students may come to realize how truly intimate an act it is to "just breathe" and that breath, our source of life, brings us closer to the world around us.

Sounding the Breath: Engaging the Sense of Pattern and Musicality

Students may not have considered that it is our breath that enables us to speak. Abram describes vowels as "sounded breath."[11] He recounts that, in approximately 1500 BCE, scribes responsible for the creation of the alphabet combined sounded and "silent" syllables or elements of language. The silent elements—what we now call vowels—provided the means to release the breath that is required to articulate a unit of sound. The vowels represent "the bodily framework or shape through which the sounded breath must flow."[12] Apart from abbreviations, every word has a vowel. Encourage students to feel in their throats, chests, and faces the different forms of "sounded breath" created by the body as they practise saying *a, e, i, o, u,* and sometimes *y.* Focus on the sounds of each differently shaped breath that escapes. Help students to understand the essential role of the escaping breath in speech and how vowels are, in some ways, its escape route: The air enters the body, is trapped in the lungs, and escapes through the sounded breath of vowels.

Playing with Air: Engaging Humour and Incongruity

On really windy days teachers might help students feel the power of the air through free play, structured games, or the use of props. Students can feel the tug of a kite string, see the impossibility of a game of badminton, or notice the influence of wind on a precisely hit golf ball. They can feel the strength required to run into a strong wind wearing different clothing (jackets/capes) or carrying different objects. *(Ever try pushing a fully open, large umbrella into the wind?)* They can try to increase or decrease their speed based on what they wear or how they position their bodies. They can see how wind influences movement on water. They can attempt to build towers of different sizes, or with objects of different weights, in different winds. For example, how many empty cans can be stacked? How many full ones?

To give students a felt sense of air's volume, they could gather in an open space and, as a group, lift a parachute high above their heads and then quickly bring it to the ground, feeling the *whump* of air filling it and thus creating air resistance that slows the descent of the parachute. Students can learn about air pressure and projectile motion by firing air cannons—a fun and safe activity.

Playing with the Wind Gods: Evoking Emotional Responses

In Greek mythology, the gods of the winds have fiery tempers and destructive force. To engage students emotionally with the topic of winds, introduce imagery that evokes the different characteristics of the four wind gods that are considered to be the children of Eos (goddess of the dawn) and Astraeus (god of the four winds). For example, picture Boreas, the dramatic north wind that was the most feared and powerful of all the winds: His white hair is frozen in razor-sharp spikes, his long beard slices through the clouds that frame his face. His cheeks, full with wind, are red and chapped. Now meet Zephyrus, the west wind, a pleasant, welcome wind. Zephyrus is young, with soft skin and a kind face. He brings with him warmth and moisture. Flowers are intertwined among the strands of hair that softly frame his gentle face. You can provide similar vivid imagery of Eurus (the east wind) and Notus (the south wind) and then encourage students to become these winds. How is each different? How would each move? Students can also discuss what the winds are today. How would they characterize these winds?

In mythology, the wind gods are often depicted as being like horses and winged. Why is this? A folk belief of the ancient Greeks was that in early spring the winds Boreas and Zephyrus took the shape of wind-formed stallions, swept down upon the female horses, and fertilized them. The animals born from these couplings became the fastest and finest horses of their kind.[13] What other wonderful stories exist about winds? What local Aboriginal narratives portray the meaning of winds? What stories can students bring to class that evoke the wonder, power, and mystery of winds?

Honouring: Celebrating Our Involvement in the World

As mentioned earlier, "Honouring" activities encourage students to demonstrate what they have learned, build upon their somatic experiences, and celebrate their awareness of their involvement in the world around them. The activities that follow suggest ways to honour precipitation, the sun, and the wind. They employ the body's tools in combination and also draw on cognitive tools—to be described in detail in future chapters—that evoke emotion and imagination as they enrich our relationships with place. They give students an opportunity to experience the weather phenomena differently and to express their new awareness in multi-modal ways.

Appreciating the Gifts of Rain

More often than not, people grumble when it rains. Discuss with students how rain is a positive thing and can be considered a "gift." What does precipitation give the earth? What are its gifts? What exists after a rainfall that didn't exist before? In what ways can we consider these changes to be gifts? Some students might think rain is more of a punishment than a gift—after all, it makes everything wet. How is wetness a gift? Without the gift of rain, there would be no growth. Animals (including humans) obviously require water to survive. For plants (including seeds), rain also brings the gift of life. What other gifts of rain can students think of? Possible examples include how rain lowers temperatures on a hot day, it cleans the air, and it provides water in aquifers.

Celebrating Rain in Songs and Poems

Students can create their own songs and poems about rain, which they can perform in honour of rain. What would be a good beat for a drizzle? What about for a downpour? What rhyming can students play with to capture some of what they feel about rain?

For older students, you could begin by introducing poems written about different aspects of weather and invite students to discuss their meaning. For example, students could examine the rich use of metaphors in the poem "Wind" by Ted Hughes (an audio version is available on YouTube). How do his metaphors contribute to students' understanding of the nature of wind? Philip Larkin's poem "Wedding Wind" (also available on YouTube) uses different metaphors. What does the wind mean for the happiness of this new bride? What metaphors for wind can students use in writing their own poems?

Acting Like a Rain God

Students can use gestures or create postures to demonstrate different forms of precipitation. Encourage them to play with words and expression (for example: tone, pitch, and speed) in ways that dramatically express different forms of precipitation. You can evoke the spirit of Zeus, the ancient Greek god of the sky and supreme ruler of all the gods, and use him as a source for dramatic re-enactments and role play.

Zeus tends to be depicted visually in ways that evoke his power and strength. Suggest that students imagine Zeus standing boldly within a startling storm of lightning, his hair blown askew in the unrelenting wind, a thunderbolt in his hand, ready to be launched at anyone who displeases him. His biceps bulge as though he is about to hurl his thunderbolt—is it *you* who have upset him? What have you done to displease him? Now invite students to imagine Zeus at rest. Although he is deep in thought, seated on a massive throne, his facial expression remains fierce. He is a force to be reckoned with. What kind of storm depicts the power and ferocity of Zeus? How might this god of rain and gatherer of clouds evoke a storm? How might he walk? How might he gather up the clouds that will unleash upon the earth his next mighty storm? Students can also demonstrate their understanding of Zeus and other mythological wind (or weather) gods through movement and gesture.

Telling Stories about Clouds and the Rain

Students can create cloud or rain stories, writing from their own perspective or perhaps that of a cloud or a mountain. (For example, writing as a mountain: "It's a rare day when I don't make contact with clouds. Whether the whispy, veil-like clouds that touch my highest peaks or the dense clouds that envelop me, I feel their touch.") What relationship might a mountain have with clouds that encompass it? What might a cloud "see" as it drifts lazily across the sky? Or what might it conceal? What might it feel about what it sees and conceals? What will happen to the earth when the rain starts to fall? What adventure begins when the first drop of rain hits the earth?

Appreciating the Gift of the Sun

Call it Amaterasu, Apollo, or Ra, our sun has many names and great significance in our lives. The sun is the source of life on earth. It symbolizes power, vitality, illumination, and glory. Not surprisingly, the sun is an important part of mythology, art, and literature in many cultures and has many symbols associated with it. You may share a variety of stories from cultures around the world about the sun's significance. If possible, representatives from local Aboriginal communities or experts on Aboriginal cultural understanding can be invited to share oral traditions about the sun and its importance for life. Students can create sun stories and design sun symbols.

They may create word images or paint with watercolours, playing with the nuances of shade and hue that this medium allows. They may use colour, pattern, or texture to visually represent their experiences with sun and heat. How might they capture the emotional significance of a warm day? What could they create that would properly honour the sun?

Collecting Shadows

One way to honour the sunshine and its life-giving effects is to conduct art activities that involve shadows. Students can use digital photography to capture the play of light and shadow around them or set out with pencil and paper to trace shadows that they find particularly beautiful. Why did they choose a particular shadow? What does it mean to them?

Celebrating Colour

As students study sunlight, they can learn about the colour-giving role of light. Students may think that the colour they see in the world around them is a feature of objects, but actually colour is closely tied to light. You might engage students' imaginations by explaining that a ray of light is like a magic wand; it brings colour to what it touches. Students may use art projects to show how the world can burst into colour on a sunny day or capture the vibrant colours that can light up the sky at dusk.

Creating Fire

Most students will know first hand what effect the sun's rays can have on human skin. Exposure to the sun's rays in the summer—particularly at midday when the sun is in its highest position in the sky—can quickly burn our skin. Thankfully, we don't actually burst into flames despite how hot we might feel. But by using a magnifying glass, we can concentrate the power of the sun's rays enough to create fire. With appropriate supervision—and discussion of the dangers of doing this activity without an adult present—students can burn designs or messages into wood using the sun's rays and a magnifying glass.

Honouring the Wind as a Creator or a Destroyer

You can encourage students to think about ways of expressing how wind is a binary opposite: it is both creator and destroyer. What evidence can they find of wind's destructive forces? The most destructive wind phenomena—cyclones, hurricanes, and tornadoes—often arrive quite mildly, gently swaying trees and branches. As they pick up speed—often very rapidly—the trees begin to bend and crack, and branches snap and fall. At full force, the trees' deep root systems are no match for such strong winds. Uprooted at their base, trees will fall, flattening houses, cars, people, and animals. Virtually anything that isn't powerfully attached to the earth is lifted and thrown, like rag dolls.

What evidence can students find of the wind as creator? For example, its kinetic energy—wind power—can be captured and converted into electricity. Ask students if they have ever seen a wind farm. Wind farms are stretches of land or sea that are wide open, where dozens to hundreds of wind turbines (windmills) harness the power of wind. Have students imagine standing in the middle of a massive tract of land where there is enough wind to support the continuous turning of these giant turbines. Above their heads stands one such turbine, taller than a telephone pole and with broad arms turning in the wind, generating clean electrical energy.

Another binary opposition that could frame student learning about wind is whisper/ scream. Have students ever experienced a violent wind? This kind of discussion can bring into focus the extremes and limits of wind-related weather. You might, for example, discuss the typical wind speed of a breeze versus a strong wind versus a hurricane. What kinds of winds occur in students' local area? Once students have a sense of the local winds, they can look for information about extreme occurrences of wind. What local records have been set for wind speed? How loud is that kind of wind? The highest wind speed that has ever been officially recorded in the world was a gust of 372 kilometres per hour (231 mph), which was recorded in 1934 on Mount Washington, New Hampshire.[14] In 1969, during Hurricane Camille, wind gusts surpassed 322 kilometres per hour (200 mph) in Biloxi, Mississippi,[15] while in 2005, the maximum wind speeds of Hurricane Katrina were measured at 225 kilometres per hour (140 mph) near Grand Isle, Louisiana.[16]

Conclusion

This chapter has described different ways to somatically engage students in learning about weather. All students possess the body's tools for learning, which include emotional responses, the body's senses, a sense of pattern and musicality, a sense of humour, and gesture. In IEE, these tools will be on educators' radar when teaching *any* topic. By being alert to your own body, you can support students in maintaining the vividness and potency that stems from making sense of the world through their bodies. When students tap into the body's tools for learning (the activeness principle) in conjunction with the many tools offered by our cultural context (the feeling principle), they gain knowledge that is emotionally and imaginatively meaningful. The next chapter addresses the third IEE principle, *place and sense of place*, which enriches students' learning by focusing on their sense of connectedness with the natural and cultural context in which they live.

CHAPTER 5

STRATEGIES FOR DEVELOPING STUDENTS' SENSE OF PLACE—A STUDY OF WEATHER

The meaningful contexts, or places, in which we dwell are *storied*. Each is shaped by the beings that currently live there, but also by those that came before and whose presence has forever shaped the context of that which we now call home. Our places—indeed *all places*—are therefore full of "ghosts," which are sometimes acknowledged through place names or distinctive features of the landscape. We are all, thus, part of a shared geographical and historical story. Stop for a moment and think about a natural or cultural context that you identify with, somewhere you have deep knowledge of and a sense of belonging or attachment to. What's the story of this place? What's your role in the story? The text that follows recounts my memories of the place where I grew up.

> I recently returned to the arbutus-filled acreage where I grew up in Saanich, British Columbia, a rural municipality outside Victoria on Vancouver Island. I ran my hand over the smooth bark of an arbutus tree that is still growing on the property, much bigger now than when I was last here. The cool, silky texture of the bark, the look of the knotted and twisting branches, and the patterning created on the leaf-strewn ground beneath the tree evoked some powerful, emotionally charged images in my mind. Growing up, we used, abused, and ultimately adored the arbutus trees sharing the land. We peeled their bark and—I now shudder to recall—carved messages onto their trunks. We also cut some of the trees down, clearing land for our driveway and home, and for running trails. We used some of their wood for heating our home. We attached a rope swing to the biggest arbutus

on the property, using it for our daring swings out over the land below. Under the arbutus trees were the paths we ran, the imposing fortresses we built, and the hiding places we felt no one would ever find. I recall being mesmerized by the soft dancing patterns cast by the sunlight as it streamed through the arbutus branches. The trees offered welcome shade in the afternoons, a canopy of broken light protecting me from the sun's rays. I often thought that their peeling bark was like my skin after too much time in the sun. At night, the arbutus leaves on twisted branches created dancing patterns against the darkening sky.

These are my memories, my stories. And yet this place—one that evokes my emotions and imagination—is populated by more than the ghosts of my family and friends. It is storied with the tales of all those that came before—including, centrally, the Saanich First Nations people who inhabited the land, who walked upon the same earth, who touched the arbutus trees, and who rested in the trees' patterned shadows. Our places are sources of mystery and magic that can be evoked in the telling of our stories. How can you evoke your students' sense of mystery about the storied nature of their places?

Engaging students with the natural and cultural contexts of their local area is a central aim of place-based education: you will want to develop students' *sense of place* and leave them *feeling* something for the contexts in which they live.[1] Why? Because this emotional connection stimulates the care and concern that are at the core of a new human-nature relationship. An emotional connection with a place can provide us with vivid proof of just how interconnected we are with the world around us. The role of the teacher in IEE is to support students in developing emotional attachments with the natural world and to enable them to experience the mystery and magic of the natural and cultural contexts in which they live. To do so requires cultivation of feeling and engagement of the body and imagination.

Human beings are place-makers; everyone everywhere makes meaning of their socio-cultural and natural contexts. We attribute meaning to the spaces of our daily lives that can come to have a profound impact on the way we understand the world, ourselves, and the relationship between the two. I am interested in the ways in which our imaginative engagement in place-making might support a stronger ecological sense of place and cultivate in students a deeper connectedness to the natural world.[2] The ways in which our imaginations contribute to the meaning we make of our local contexts are known as *place-making cognitive tools*.[3]

You may be thinking that some of the previous examples of imaginative ecological activities also support sense of place. In truth, this third principle of IEE is not totally distinct from the previous two (feeling and activeness), but it introduces some place-making cognitive tools not previously discussed. It is important to remember that the three principles of IEE—feeling, activeness, and sense of place—interconnect and are most effective when woven together.

Imaginative Engagement in Place-Making

In an imaginative ecological approach to teaching, increased knowledge of place (including, for example, knowledge of flora and fauna, geological and cultural history, and so on) is paired with affective engagement. In other words, learning activities are shaped to tap into the emotional and imaginative ways in which students make meaning of their contexts. So, in addition to the cognitive tools that evoke feeling, imaginative ecological educators also employ students' place-making cognitive tools. Our sense of relation, an innate desire to connect with the world around us, is arguably the most important place-making tool of all.[4]

Children develop a sense of place through the formation of emotional attachments to particular features of their immediate environments and to particular processes or rituals they experience on a frequent basis. So, for example, a teddy bear or "blankie" contributes to a child's sense of self and world, offering a needed source of comfort and security. Children often grow very attached to these "permanent" objects in their environments, which are often items they select. (You may have noticed how often one "stuffy" slowly disintegrates with years of loving and other, perfectly lovable bears and bunnies are barely touched.) Young children's senses of self and place are often blurred because they experience a highly participatory form of engagement in the world. Shared processes or rituals also contribute to a child's sense of belonging in a place, to the meaning of the place and what sets it apart in the child's mind. For example, family pancake breakfasts on weekend mornings, a "hug, kiss, and a high-five" before bed, or a favourite story each night are rituals that help children develop a sense of belonging. In the adult world, shared rituals or customs continue to contribute to a sense of place and a sense of belonging (for example, raising a flag or participating in a Thanksgiving Day meal).

Place-Making Activities for Young Children

The following questions can help you think about ways to imaginatively engage young children in place-making activities:

- How can students learn about the topic in a way that engages them emotionally and imaginatively with some aspect of the natural world around them?
- How does the topic connect to the local environment? What does it mean *here*?
- What processes or patterns can students participate in as part of their learning about this topic?
- What shared rituals can be established?

When teaching young children who are predominantly oral language users, you will want to afford them opportunities to develop emotional attachments to particular aspects of the natural environment that include objects as well as processes or patterns. Strich describes how the "sit spot"—or what is also described as the "special spot" activity—can support this kind of engagement.[5] Strich uses SPOT as an acronym to refer to four features typical of this learning activity: **S**ensory engagement, **P**erceptions, **O**bservations, and **T**elling, or a final sharing of what has been learned. He notes that benefits of the SPOT activity include increased opportunities for personal growth, reflection, engagement with place, and the development of attentiveness required for scientific inquiry.[6]

Encourage young children to select a place in the natural environment that they find inviting. This location will be theirs in the sense that they will be given ample opportunity to return to it and experience it at various times of day and throughout the school year. They will come to know it more intimately than anyone else will. Children will go to this special place to study and observe various meteorological phenomena, as well as to think, reflect, rest, draw, or play. Over time, and with frequent opportunities to linger in this specific spot, this place may come to be a sort of "safe haven" for the children. It may become a home away from home.

You can engage students' imaginative interest in processes and patterns by guiding the kind of observations they make in these places. For example, invite students to notice how their special place changes in appearance (including sound, smell, and touch) throughout the course of a day. Who comes and who goes in this place? What does a day (or hour) in the life of a particular spot look like in October as compared to in February or June? By drawing students' attention to daily patterns in their special place, they can deepen their understanding of what this place means. They may develop emotional connections to the subtle and not-so-subtle changes in their special spot. Over time, each child can place "roots" or establish emotional meanings in his or her place, ultimately developing a sense of rootedness in place through deepened knowledge and emotional connection.

You can support students' creative engagement with place by introducing imaginary scenarios. For example, ask students to imagine exploring a forest and discovering, neatly tucked into the base of a hill or amongst the roots of an old tree perhaps, a tiny front door. What would they do? Knock? Run? Invite students to imagine what it would be like to come upon the home of a talking rabbit with a carefully manicured garden beside a miniature mailbox. What might be behind the door?

Place-Making Activities for Students of All Ages

It is not only young children who value a shared sense of process or who benefit from a collective sense of place. One way to celebrate a school-wide sense of place and community, across age and grade levels, is to establish common processes or rituals for beginning the school day that focus on belonging. For example, students could spend some time welcoming each other, the place, or the weather so that everyone can acknowledge their membership in a community of learning that includes their peers, teachers/teacher aides, and the more-than-human world. One form of welcome could be through a shared song or chant that honours the place and all its inhabitants. Following the singing, you could guide students in welcoming the day through different breathing exercises—drawing attention to the air as the shared medium connecting everyone with the natural world—or other activities that draw attention to the body and its immersion in place. Alternatively, each student might go to his or her special place to welcome it and all its inhabitants to the day.

How might students come together to represent this storied place? How might a mosaic of symbols and signs representing how each child understands or experiences his or her special spot be used to create a class flag? The day could begin with the raising of the flag and could end with its lowering. Similar kinds of rituals might be established with the aim of drawing attention to place and building a sense of shared identity in the place. How might the class bid each other—and the natural world—farewell at the end of each day? How does one say goodbye to a place overnight?

Place-Making Activities for Older Students

The following questions can help you think about ways to imaginatively engage older children in place-making activities:

- What aspect of the topic might be learned in a way that affords students the opportunity to explore the natural world around them?
- How might learning about the topic support a sense of belonging in the natural environment?

Older students imaginatively engage in place-making in ways that reflect their growing sense of an independent, separate reality. As they internalize the tools of written language, or literacy, they begin to lose the sense of participation in the world that characterizes the understanding of oral-language users. As discussed previously, students may develop a growing interest in the extremes and limits of reality as well as the heroic aspects of the real world and its human dimensions, including an interest in ingenuity, success, revolt, and idealism. Literate students imaginatively engage with place by creating special places such as forts, dens, or hideouts. The creation (or discovery) of special places supports their attempts to deal with a new sense of reality by offering a secure place in which they can have autonomy and from which they can creatively—and safely—explore wider social, cultural, or natural contexts.

You can support place-making and creative engagement in context by letting students explore the natural world around them. Students may be invited to explore a certain area and find a location that attracts their attention. What invites them? What place draws them? Where would they like to settle in and do some thinking? Reading? Writing? Alternatively, ask students to imagine that they are being pursued by something dreadfully scary. Where would they hide? How would they hide? Throughout the weather unit, students can be given opportunities to create shelters of various kinds. They might imagine a scenario where extreme weather conditions are moving in. Working in groups, can students build a shelter to keep the whole group dry and warm?

Students could establish weather stations or lookouts from which to make their observations about different weather phenomena and to collect weather data over time. They might create different symbols to depict the uniqueness of each particular location, then map and frequently visit these places as part of their meteorological studies. Building on the "special spot" activity described in this section, older students might be encouraged to map their own and their peers' special spots. They might develop a visual sense of where each of their classmates is "rooted" and may come to associate different places in the natural world with different classmates. They can map the routes between all of their classmates' special places. Mapping can be used in multiple ways to develop a sense of place and also help students express what they feel about place.[7]

The development of an emotional attachment to place takes time. It is crucial to remember that it is only through *ongoing* contact with a place that students can come to know it and care for it. To facilitate long-term engagement with the local natural and cultural context and to afford students opportunities that will call upon all of their imaginative learning tools, you may want to consider including in the curriculum two kinds of long-term projects: an independent study of a place-based topic or a collaborative (school-wide) place-based project.

Independent Place-Based Investigations

One way to support place-based investigations over time is by giving students an opportunity for long-term and in-depth study of a single topic that connects to their local natural environment. The aim of this type of project is for each student to become an "expert" on one aspect of the local natural world; he or she would soon know more about the topic than anyone else in the class or even in the school. Each student has the opportunity to develop a strong sense of connection with a particular aspect of place.

One way to shape such work is by using the model that Egan calls the Learning in Depth or LiD program.[8] In LiD, students have an opportunity to gain a depth of knowledge that is unmatched by any other feature of their schooling. Students are assigned topics for individual investigation early in their schooling that they are then supported in studying for the remainder of their years at school. An ecologically oriented LiD program would allow students the opportunity to learn in depth about something in their local contexts. Topics might include spiders, apples, wood, weather, mountains, light, fish, ponds and lakes, mushrooms, trees, and so on. For approximately one hour a week, students can freely investigate their topics. They decide what they want to learn next. They decide what aspects of the topic to pursue. They share their learning informally with peers and the teacher on a regular basis and, once a year, participate in a larger and more formal "knowledge fair" in which all students present what they have learned about their topics.

The premise of this approach is that the more students know about their topic, the more knowledge they will gain about the place and the more they can become emotionally and imaginatively engaged. It brings together the two main aspects of sense of place: knowledge and affective engagement. Whatever topic students investigate becomes a powerful source of their connection with place and one piece of their growing knowledge base about where they are in the world. In the LiD model, students' investigations are part of the regular curriculum but they are ungraded. Students are afforded support once a week to investigate their topics in ways that they choose, but they never feel the pressure of evaluation.

Offering an ungraded opportunity to learn is one way to encourage students to enjoy learning. Schools generally don't provide enough activities that allow students to enjoy learning for learning's sake. More often than not, students come to associate school and learning with stress or boredom. By allowing students the time to become "expert," to connect to place in a way that does not involve the pressure of so much else they do in school, teachers can support place-making and the pleasure of learning.

School-wide Collaborative Projects

School-wide collaborative projects are another option for supporting place-making. In this model, all students contribute to the creation of a product that reflects an aspect of the natural or cultural world. Teachers can weave the regular curriculum into a school-wide project, creating place-based interdisciplinary learning opportunities. One model for this kind of initiative is the Whole School Project, or WSP, in which students in a school participate in a three-year investigation of a topic. While a WSP need not focus on the local natural and cultural context—as Egan notes in his book describing this program[9]—focusing on the immediate environment can be an excellent option. Egan suggests, for example, that an entire student body take on the investigation of a few blocks around the school—the flora and fauna, what is underground, what is above ground, and so on. What can students learn about this particular piece of the planet? If the math curriculum at a certain grade level includes the study of surface area, those students can investigate this topic in the context of the WSP; they learn both about surface area and something specific about the project. Similarly, a biology class might look at local flora once every week or so.

For a WSP to succeed, teachers must coordinate the investigations. They need to decide, for example, how investigations will integrate the curriculum, thereby supporting the fulfillment of mandated learning outcomes. They must also decide what the final product for the project will be and how each group of students will contribute. What will be created and what features will students in grades 1, 2, 8, or 9 contribute? Following the WSP model, a final product is displayed and shared with the community.

A collaborative, locally focused investigation offers IEE students additional means to develop in-depth knowledge and emotional connections with place. Over time and through imaginative engagement, students can come to notice the storied nature of the local natural and cultural contexts where they live. They can learn about the ghosts with whom they share the land. They can learn about the living entities—calculating quantities of butterflies, flies, or aphids; exploring transient and indigenous bird and insect populations; counting exotic and indigenous plant species, and so on—that share their places. Because shared projects of this type provide a goal for students to work towards across grades and age levels, these projects add to a school's sense of identity and, simultaneously, to students' sense of identity within the school. Whole school projects can therefore be a powerful way to cultivate and sustain a sense of community in a school—community that connects students, teachers, parents, community members, *and* the natural and cultural world.

Conclusion

Through long-term and place-focused projects, either individual or collaborative, students can make powerful interdisciplinary connections. They come to realize that the world doesn't exist in the compartmentalized way that we tend to represent it in schools. Open the doors and students can learn that math, science, social studies, and art are all aspects of a bigger picture, of the living world of which they are part. In addition to employing many of the cognitive tools described so far that engage the imagination, what is perhaps most valuable in place-based projects is that these activities increase students' knowledge of where they are in the world at a time when they are figuring out who they are. With more knowledge of place and the enriched imaginative capacity an IEE approach to teaching can provide, students can open up to the mystery and wonder of the world around them. The natural places around them can contribute in subtle ways to students' identity formation and can begin to take hold of their hearts.

CHAPTER 6

USING IEE PRINCIPLES TO SUPPORT READING AND WRITING

Being able to track—to "read" or make sense of the many signs of life in the landscape—was, at one time, a requirement for people's immediate survival. Rewind 2,000 years: If you didn't find your quarry, you and your people didn't eat. Fast-forward to the present day: Now, most people don't have to rely on accurately identifying spoor (indication of an animal's presence, such as tracks, signs, and trails) to put food on the table. However, the art of tracking has continued significance in the cultivation of ecological understanding, environmental planning, and law enforcement. Today, we are much more likely to be able to read the written word than the signs and symbols of the natural world.

Overview of Literacy Unit: Chapters 6 and 7

You may be wondering how human survival and tracking are connected with literacy. Tracking is a metaphor through which to imaginatively engage students in learning to read and write the signs of the alphabet and develop other literacy skills. This chapter and chapter 7 describe a range of place-based, ecologically sensitive activities designed to support you in developing the literacy skills of your students while fulfilling the mandated curriculum. This chapter begins with background information on how this literacy unit was developed, describes how mythic and romantic story forms or narrative structures were used to shape instruction on tracking and literacy, and concludes with ongoing activities that connect students' literacy development with somatic engagement and place-making. Chapter 7 provides tracking and literacy activities designed for three different natural places: a riverside, a wood, and a riverbed. These activities can be adapted to your local context. Chapter 7 concludes with activities that allow students to bring the story form or narrative of tracking and literacy to a celebratory closure.

The place-based tracking and literacy unit outlined in these two chapters has three pedagogical aims. The first aim is to show students how reading the *world* (tracking) and reading the *word* (alphabetic literacy) broaden human consciousness in distinctively different ways and contribute to two different understandings of the human-nature relationship. Tracking represents a kind of engagement that may bring us into closer relationship with the world around us, whereas literacy may leave us dislocated from the natural world. By drawing students' attention to the distinctive way alphabetic literacy engages us in the world and juxtaposing it with the tools of orality and the heightened somatic awareness of tracking, students may recognize how the various technologies we use to understand the world also shape the world we see.

The second aim of this unit is to support students in developing a sense of place. The suggested activities engage place-making and other imaginative tools that can nurture students' sense of immersion in a living world. These activities can easily be adapted to meet the needs of students in a variety of contexts.

The third aim of the unit is for students to become able writers and readers. The activities provide many opportunities for them to fulfill the kinds of mandated curriculum objectives for literacy that are similar in many jurisdictions. Along with the proposed activities, students of all ages and abilities should be given opportunities to read during each school day. Their literacy skills can be nurtured through guided reading (for new readers) and independent reading (for developing readers) of a variety of texts linked to unit themes, as well as books of their own choosing.

Background on the Development of the Unit

Planning this unit departed in two main ways from the kind of teaching practice I was trained in.

The first departure was that the literacy objectives did not direct my planning. That is, I did not work backward from the features of literacy I wanted to teach and design activities that would attend to each one. Rather, I began by reviewing features of literacy my students needed to learn. Then I thought about the emotional significance of literacy. *What is the story on literacy?* What is it about literacy that can evoke students' sense of wonder? Then I turned to the cognitive tools I knew my students would be using to make sense of the world around them and that I could employ to evoke their emotions in learning.

To address the different forms of imaginative engagement of new and more experienced readers, I developed two different story forms or narrative ways of shaping instruction on tracking and literacy: one "mythic" and the other "romantic."

The mythic story form is designed to engage the imaginations of new readers (approximately K–Grade 2/3) and employs the cognitive tools of oral language. For these students, learning preliminary techniques for tracking can make them more aware of their surroundings and develop the kind of sensory awareness that can make the invisible become visible. Students will begin to "read" the signs around them, recognizing the multiple ways in which an outdoor space and its inhabitants communicate with them. An increased alertness to place will bring students closer to the world of plants and wildlife that surrounds them. The written word can also bring the invisible into view, so activities are included that will enrich students' recognition and use of the symbols of alphabetic literacy.

The romantic story form or narrative on tracking and literacy is designed to engage the imaginations of developing readers (approximately Grades 3–7) and employs cognitive tools of written language. This unit can enrich their literacy skills through developing their vocabularies and creative writing skills. It also aims to develop perceptual acuteness and, correspondingly, a more sophisticated and trained level of literacy. An able tracker observes the world with an acute level of discernment; the track is a window into the life of an animal.

The second departure was that, unlike most curricular units, this unit is connected to and designed for use in a particular place: Cliff Park, Maple Ridge, a rural community near Vancouver, BC. I chose three locations in Cliff Park that influenced and inspired my thinking and planning: the shores of Kanaka Creek, a cottonwood forest, and alongside sandstone cliffs in the upper riverbed. However, the activities provided here can help you develop imaginative place-based activities for your own context. Ideally you will have access to one or more of the generic locations described in chapter 7.

I strongly urge all IEE teachers to engage with place themselves. IEE is a place-focused pedagogy and it requires the involvement of teachers with an interest in, or an interest in developing, a sense of place wherever they teach. If you wish to awaken your students to the wonders of the places in which they live, you need to engage with place yourself, letting the natural world evoke your imagination and letting place be your teacher. The suggested activities in this unit are primarily a guide or stepping-off point for your own place-based and place-inspired literacy instruction.

Part I: Teaching Tracking and Literacy through the Story Form or Narrative Structure

A Mythic Approach: Framing the teaching of literacy for students in K– Grades 2/3

Note: Suggestions for what you might do appear in *italic* text in parentheses.

COGNITIVE TOOLS EMPLOYED:
☑ Binary opposites (visible/invisible; meaningful/ meaningless)
☑ Mental imagery
☑ Metaphor
☑ Sense of mystery and puzzles

(Begin by asking students the following kinds of questions as a way of weaving an imaginative context for your literacy lessons.) What does it mean to be alone? Have you ever been in a natural place like this one and felt completely alone? Imagine you are all alone in this place. Close your eyes. Try to let the images you have in your mind of your friends standing around you slip away. Keeping your eyes closed, pretend that your eyes are not closed; pretend that they are actually OPEN and that you are the only one here. Pretend that the sound of my voice is your own, inner voice. Think about your breath. Breathe in slowly and deeply. *(Try to describe as vividly as possible what you and your students are sensing in place. What follows is what I experienced as I immersed myself in my natural context. Depending on where you are, you may or may not have access to a forested area such as I describe here. However, playgrounds, local parks, or gardens offer wonderful opportunities for evoking students' mental imagery of place.)*

Smell the faint scent of wet ground, of moss, of bark. Feel the air against your cheek. You are feeling the breath of the forest. Listen for the sound of the flowing river. Against the constant sound of the water in motion, notice the sound of the water bubbling up against obstacles in the river. Now look—with closed eyes—for the messages coming from the place that surrounds you. You are not alone. You are surrounded by life but you do not yet know how to recognize the signs. What signs of life do you hear around you? What signs of life do you see? *(Instruct students to open their eyes. Encourage them to explore a little. Have them come back and be ready to describe some of the signs they noticed visually. They may begin to collect the visual signs by making sketches in their journals. Focus on other senses. For example, spend time talking about the signs of life they heard—can they recreate the sounds? What did they smell? What did they feel? What did they choose to touch?)*

(Next you might take a stick and mark the letters R E A D in the dirt. Ask the students some questions about these odd markings.) What are these squiggles? Do they mean anything to you? Where might you find groups of squiggles like this? *(Bring the conversation around to the idea of squiggles being letters, groups of squiggles being words, and collections of these being found all around us but especially in books).* These are human symbols—another kind of sign. Who knows their letters? Who knows the whole alphabet? Who can sing it? Who can sign it? *(Sing it! Sign it!)* Letters reveal messages—and only those people who really know all about letters can read these messages.

(You can now extend the notion of markings—or squiggles—to those in nature.) Have you ever noticed that the earth is covered with marks, scrawls, squiggles, shapes, and so on? We are surrounded by all sorts of signs that communicate important meanings to those who understand those signs. What shapes, traces, lines, or patterns do you notice? You might think about this place, this park, as a book. If you learn to read signs, you can enter into it, just as learning to read words lets you enter into the story in a book. Children living here long ago learned how to read the signs of life around them from their elders, and with this knowledge they were able to survive. What did they need to survive? How did being able to read the signs of the natural world help them to survive? You are going to learn to read these same signs: you will learn to track just as the children did who lived here long ago. You are also going to learn to read the signs and symbols that come with the alphabet—two very different kinds of "reading" that will require you to do lots of exploring.

Until you start to recognize natural signs or human signs (the squiggles we call the alphabet), they are just squiggles. Until you begin to learn to identify the different letters and to make sense of groups of letters, or words, they are meaningless. Starting today you will begin to learn how to read the messages present in the world around you—those of animals and humans. Right now, you may not recognize them, so they are meaningless. Reading the signs of life in this place—what we will call tracking—allows you to learn more about the animals that live here, the plants that grow here, and the ways in which we are all connected to the natural world. Learning to read words will allow you to expand what you know, enter into other people's experiences, share your own experiences, and connect with each other. When you learn to read, groups of squiggles will become stories that can take you to places and times you never imagined. When you learn to write, you can share your deepest thoughts, feelings, and secrets. If you are a skilled tracker and reader, you realize you are never completely alone. You can identify the signs of animal life all around you that, to the untrained eye, ear, and nose, often remain invisible. If you are a reader, you can engage with other people even if they are not present. *(This is a good time to make a dramatic stretching sound.)* Can you feel your world getting bigger?

A Romantic Approach: Framing the teaching of literacy for students in Grades 3–7

(The following story form represents one way to weave an imaginative context for literacy development with older students.) SCAT!! Sometimes wildlife leaves us obvious messages of its presence. What are some very obvious indications that animals have been here? What might you see? Skilled and experienced trackers see what does not exist to the unskilled eye, ear, and nose. Tracking involves a level of discernment and attention to detail that most people do not have. Trackers are detectives of the forest. It is this attention to detail gained through using all of the senses that allows trackers to notice signs that an untrained person would miss. For example, slight changes in branch positioning can indicate an animal's direction of movement; an overturned stone or slight patterning in the soil can reveal a clue to an animal's location.

COGNITIVE TOOLS EMPLOYED:

☑ Heroic qualities (discernment; attention to detail)

☑ Humanizing meaning

☑ Extremes of experience and limits of reality

☑ Sense of wonder

☑ Mental imagery

(Here you may want to introduce the Shadow Wolves task force.) Since 1972, a group of Native American trackers referred to as Shadow Wolves have worked for American law enforcement to chase smugglers on tribal lands along the border between Arizona and Mexico. Every Shadow Wolf member is an expert in "cutting for sign," the traditional tracking skills used by Native American tribes to hunt game. This method includes examining footprints, noticing disturbed vegetation, and identifying minute details such as strands of thread on tree branches. The depth of a track or print can indicate the size of an animal or the weight of a person. Despite the availability of modern tracking technologies, Shadow Wolf trackers, who come from nine different tribes, continue to use the traditional tracking techniques of their ancestors. Individually, they have a phenomenal ability to track and catch their target, calling in their team to join them, as would a pack of wolves, to apprehend illegal migrants or drug smugglers on American land. They use GPS locaters, high-powered radios, ATVs, and other modern tools, but it is their tracking skills and their feel for the hidden canyons, caves, and seasonal watering holes that make them formidable counter-narcotics agents.[1]

(Alert your students to the kind of attention required of trackers—an attention we routinely do not have.) Have you ever zoned out and then realized it? Have you ever felt like you're on autopilot? By this I mean, following the daily routines of life—getting to school, for example—without really being aware of what you are doing? Tracking requires you to be awake and alert. No zoning out and no autopilot. Trackers open up their senses to the world around them, letting the sights, sounds, smells, tastes, and textures of a place wash over them, employing their senses to learn about the quarry they pursue. With time, they come to anticipate and predict where the animal might move next, leaving a trail towards a predicted destination. Trackers enter into a relationship with the animal. It is

through close attention, focused alertness, and studying an animal over time that trackers can begin to identify with the animal. This is when anticipation and predication of animal movement becomes possible. Abram describes this kind of alertness in native hunters. *(You might read the following passage aloud to your students, asking them to imagine being such a hunter.)*

> If a native hunter is tracking, alone, in the forest, and a whooping cry reaches his ears from the leafy canopy, he will likely halt in his steps, silencing his breathing in order to hear that sound, when it comes again, more precisely. His eyes scan the cacophony of branches overhead with an unfocused gaze, attentive to minute movements on the periphery of the perceptual field. A slight rustle of branches draws his eyes into a more precise focus, his attention now restricted to a small patch of canopy, yet still open, questioning, listening. When the cry comes again, the eyes, led by the ears, swiftly converge upon the source of that sound, and suddenly a monkey's form becomes evident, half-hidden from the leaves, its tail twirled around a limb, its body poised, watching.[2]

There is another way in which we can engage with the world, one that enlarges even more the scope of the world we can come to know. Can anyone guess what I'm talking about? It's a technology that human beings have invented. *(Discussion.)* I'm referring to the technology of the written word: alphabetic literacy—reading and writing. You may never have thought about written language as a technology, but it is in fact a very powerful technology. Alphabetic literacy—being able to read and write—broadens our understanding. It changes the way we engage with the world around us.

We are going to learn to read the world and words with increased attention, skill, and accuracy. Can anyone think of how tracking and reading are similar? How are they different? *(Discussion.)* They are similar because both involve recognizing signs, symbols, and messages. What is different is the kind of attention *word* reading as opposed to *world* reading (tracking) requires. When you read the world, all of your senses need to be wide awake. Remember the native hunter? It is only through use of all of your body's senses and learning tools that you can get closer to the natural world—close enough to directly encounter and relate to it. When you read words, you rely mostly on your vision and engage with the world indirectly, vicariously. Both ways of reading, however, broaden the world you know. We're going to learn to track, read, and write at the same time. You will develop a rich vocabulary and will be able to use words to vividly and creatively evoke what you learn about this place and its animal inhabitants.

Part II: Ongoing Activities for Supporting Activeness and Place-Making

Let us now consider some activities that can support the body's engagement in learning and place-making on an ongoing basis. The following descriptions are purposefully brief; they are meant to describe and inspire some ideas, not prescribe specific lessons. The needs and skills of your students will provide the specifics. Using a field journal would be helpful for all of the activities provided. In journals students can freely document their engagement in these tracking activities and can include scribbles, sketches, detailed drawings, ideas, notes, and more developed writing. Students should also have ongoing access to a range of reading materials that build on the themes in this unit as well as topics they choose independently.

Activities for New Readers: Students in K–Grades 2/3

The following six activities develop place-making skills for new readers.

Apprenticing to place

Encourage students to look around the local natural area, exploring it for a short time. Ask them to find a location they would like to return to on an ongoing basis. They should find their own spot, away from their friends, if possible. Explain that they will be paying close attention to this place and will, over time, come to learn a great deal about it. Students will likely come to feel a sense of calm in their special places and may choose to return to them to engage in other learning activities. Encourage them to think about their special place as a teacher; their special place has a story to tell them. What is the story? You can guide students in engaging all of their senses as they learn about their special spot.

Ask: *What is this place showing you? What can you feel here? See? Smell? Hear? What changes here from day to day? What changes here throughout the day?* The aim of this activity is to nurture students' emotional attachments with particular natural locations. Their understanding of what makes their place unique can serve as a basis for many language arts–based activities.

When students have begun to engage with their place in sensory ways, they may begin to document in a field journal what they are noticing. You can easily adapt the kinds of entries students make in their journals for this and other activities in order to meet their differing skill levels and to fulfill different prescribed learning outcomes for literacy (e.g., from basic letter formations to words, simple sentences, stories, and so on).

Local heroes

Ask students to choose an animal or insect found in the local natural area to learn as much about as they can. How does this animal or insect act? Move? Communicate? What's funny about it? Can they create some jokes about it? What can this animal or insect do that makes it special in the animate world? What can it do that a person can't? What role does it play in this place? What is its story? In role as reporters for a local paper, students can explain why their animal or insect is a local hero.

Students can use journals for drawing; labelling; identifying key vocabulary in relation to the animal or insect's shape, size, movements, eating and sleeping habits, nesting habits; and so on. They can create hero cards and/or write short "books" on their chosen creatures. Knowledge gained through observation of their animal or insect in place may be supported with research online and in magazines and books.

What's growing on?

Ask students to choose a plant growing in their place to observe and document. What makes this plant unique? What does it look like throughout the day or at different times of the year? How does it change? How does it survive? How does this plant reproduce? Does it grow upright or close to the ground? How does it move in a wind? What sound represents this plant? Does it have a scent? What's the story on this plant?

In addition to the kinds of literacy activities mentioned in the previous activity, students can combine their expert knowledge of different plants with their animal studies. They can use informational, descriptive, and creative writing as they provide an ongoing account of a local plant. Students may also design storyboards or cartoon strips to tell the stories of the plant, animal, or insect that they are observing.

Colour watch

This activity focuses students' investigation of place on colour. Teachers can assign different colours to students early in the year and encourage them to become colour watchers and, ultimately, colour connoisseurs. How many naturally occurring shades of brown, green, yellow, or red can they find? What are some extremely different shades of the same colour? Students can seek out various colours outside and then, as a group, create a visual rainbow of natural colour. If possible, students could collect digital images of their colours across the seasons. They can also collect physical samples—leaves, mosses, bark, berries. After a very short time, "brown" will not be an adequate description, nor will "light brown" or "dark brown." Students can create their own names for unique colours— the more exotic and nuanced the better. As they organize and classify the colours, naming them with evocative names, they will develop a rich vocabulary. As a final activity tied to literacy development, students can write descriptive sentences that evoke the shades and hues of the colours they have been studying.

Change detectives

Come to class in role as a detective—a change detective. (Ahead of time you could research real-life people whose work involves noticing and documenting ecological change of various kinds. Consider introducing this activity for students as if you are this person.) Enlist students as detectives on the lookout for change. In order to notice change, they need to be on high sensory alert, becoming acutely aware of their plant and animal neighbours. What evidence can they find of something becoming bigger? Of something becoming smaller? Of something that is helping something else? Of something that is becoming more complex? Of something that is becoming simpler? Can they find an example of a change in smell? Sound? Texture? Students may work together to identify and report on the changes they see. This may lead to a discussion of what causes these changes.

Students can monitor how the plant or animal they are studying looks, sounds, smells, or feels different over time. They can seek changes in pattern (visual, tactile, olfactory patterns) and document the changes in their journals on a daily or weekly basis. They can describe how the plant or animal connects with other features of the natural world around it—how it is part of a larger whole. Finally, they may use descriptive or creative writing to express their emotional responses to their discoveries of change.

Sensory training

The sensory engagement required of the tracker is much more acute than what most people are capable of in the modern world. For this reason, it might be useful to include some sensory training. Van Matre describes a program for developing students' senses and feeling of emotional connection with the natural world that can serve as a guide-line for the activities in this part of the unit.[3] All the activities work in different ways to develop students' senses and evoke their emotions and imaginations. The three dimen-sions Van Matre identifies as part of sensory training focus on developing students' senses and increasing their alertness to patterns and wholes.

To sharpen the senses, guide your students through activities that help them to focus on smells, textures, tastes, sights, and sounds. For example, give them an apple each and ask them to observe it closely.[4] What colours are on it? What different markings does it have? What does the skin or stem look like through a magnifying glass? Next students can focus on the feel of the apple. How does the top or bottom of the stem feel different from the skin? How does the apple feel different to the fingers, toes, or forearm? Encourage your students to rub their hands together or clap them vigorously and then feel the apple: How does the apple feel now? How does its weight feel to the fingers? Guide students to focus on the apple's smell and its taste. They can chew it deliberately, focusing on the feel of the apple in the mouth and on the tongue. They can notice its taste as the apple's juices are released by chewing.

To train your students in seeking patterns, they might use a magnifying glass to focus on one particular aspect of an apple and describe it in minute detail, or they might look for patterns of texture or colour on its skin. In nature, they might look for particular arrangements of shapes or lines.

To help them perceive wholes, encourage your students to look at the broader picture. For example, expand the study of an apple to the tree where it grows: What new meaning is brought to the apple when it is examined in this way? Where does the apple fit in the context of the tree? Where does the tree fit in the context of the yard, orchard, or community? You can introduce activities in which students take a broader or more expansive look at the world in general. For example, they might:

- focus on the horizon, noticing what is below and above it;
- focus on negative space, such as the "empty" space between the branches of a tree or behind a flower, rather than on the branches or flower itself;
- survey where they are and collect all the details they can from various perspectives; and
- use all their senses to observe their surroundings as completely as possible.

In these activities, students learn that the tiniest objects are as important to understanding context as are the largest.

As students participate in sensory training, they can engage in many different language arts activities. For example, they can write poetry that honours the apple or any other object they have focused on. Students can combine sketching with words, creating word pictures. In word pictures, an image is created using words written in different ways, shapes, and sizes. At first glance, the sketch looks like a shape or image, but up close one can see that it consists entirely of words.

Activities for Developing Readers: Students in Grades 3–7

The following seven activities can enhance place-making skills for developing readers.

Calling all phenologists! Becoming ecological monitors

Phenology is the study of change. This activity engages students as phenologists. Their task is to examine changes in place through ongoing and systematic ecological monitoring. Since full sensory engagement is required to notice subtle changes, students will benefit by having participated in some of the sensory training described in the previous section.

As ecological monitors, older students can do more sophisticated tracking of a plant or animal than younger students, but teachers should always encourage them to somatically engage with the topic by heightening their senses, exploring patterns, and identifying wholes. Student phenologists should be equipped with the proper gear: gardening gloves, measurement tools such as rulers, field journals, pencils, and digital cameras (if possible). They can organize the data they collect into charts, tables, graphs, and so on. Quantitative data about size, shape, distribution, movement, and so on can be analyzed in multiple ways that develop different mathematical skills. The digital photographs, videos, or sound recordings they collect can be stored online for discussion in science or other classes. Students can use these photos, videos, or sound recordings in multiple art projects or as the basis for creative writing. You can encourage students to refine their descriptions of change by using precise vocabulary and different styles of writing.[5]

Conducting biodiversity surveys

In this activity, students will create appropriate tools for detecting, assessing, and recording different plant and animal species in the playground, park, or other outdoor places. They can compile data about the amount and diversity of plant and animal life, and give individual presentations on particular plants or animals. As a class, students may start a collection of species. You might challenge students to identify and learn about two or three more species of plants and animals that have not yet been identified. This type of investigation will require close observation and full sensory engagement if students are to differentiate between species. As they learn about the unique names, features, growth habits, and so on of different species, they can begin to develop a classification system in their journals. As in the previous activity, students will collect, organize, analyze, and present the information they gain about local biodiversity. Students may invite their parents and community members to celebrate the diversity of life they discover through a forum or exhibit. Students will be the experts; they can teach.

Collecting shapes and shadows

This activity combines creative writing with art. Students will explore the natural shapes and patterns created by light by collecting as many different shadows as they can in some part of the playground, or other outdoor space. Shadows are sometimes cast through an intricate canopy, so the shapes will be endlessly varied. Students can trace the shapes in their field journals or use digital photography to collect shadows. How would they describe the shapes they collect? Which ones do they prefer and why? What would they name their shadows? Through journal prompts you may invite students to describe in sensory ways the context in which each shadow was found. You may also challenge students to investigate more scientific knowledge of light and shadows. How and why do shadows created by the sun change throughout the day and why do they eventually disappear at night? Students may also do some special homework, such as collecting at night the shadows cast by a particularly bright moon.

Collecting (post)cards

We've all received or sent postcards. People often choose a specific postcard because they feel the card depicts something of the place they are in. In this activity, students will explore the idea of postcards as representations of place. Ask them to think about how to represent to others the "feel" of the playground or a local park. Students can begin by taking a photograph of something in the local natural world and making it into a traditional postcard. Then they can write the postcard to someone, describing why they feel this image represents the place.

Next, the students can focus on sounds. Their challenge is to describe the sound of the place in as vivid a way as possible so whoever is listening will develop a vivid mental image of the sound of the playground or park. Using highly descriptive language, they will create auditory postcards and can "play" them for classmates. Students could do similar representations by identifying smells and creating olfactory cards, or evoking textures for tactile cards. Their writing about each of these dimensions will require a refined use of language and a rich vocabulary. Teachers can expect to see a great diversity in the sensory cards students create, illustrating the wide diversity of experiences in place.

Tales from the trail

In this activity, enlist students as travel writers whose job it is to write about their experiences of the natural world in a way that would draw others to the place.[6] Students can explore a local outdoor space and write about it as if for a travel or tourism paper or webpage. You may contact a local tourism organization to see if it would publish exemplary pieces of your students' work, or you may consider starting a blog to post their writing. Encourage your students to reflect by asking them the following kinds of questions:

- How does the written description of the experience differ from the experience itself?
- How might someone reading about the place in a different location and time experience it?
- How different is reading about a place from hearing about it in a face-to-face encounter?
- Why is it that two people who share the same experience often describe it in such different ways?

Catching concepts

What does an ecological concept like "interdependence" look like in this place? What does "complexity" look like? Teachers can challenge students to "catch" real-world demonstrations of ecological concepts through digital photography or sketching. How does the photographic image or sketch differ from the real thing? Can students support the image with descriptive writing that brings the image or sketch closer to the actual thing? How does a written text help to articulate the concept?

Breaking news!

In this activity, students become news reporters. Their task is to create an engaging account of a natural phenomenon in the local area. You might begin by discussing as a class what makes for a good story. Encourage your students to then employ these features in their stories.

They can choose any topic relating to the local natural world (e.g., a change they have observed, something about the diversity of local life, information on a local plant or animal) and shape it in a way that will engage an audience. What's the story on the recent changes in the water level? What's the story on the new tracks along the riverbank? What's the story on the fallen trees? Students can provide written and oral reports from the place—local news about ongoing developments, breaking news, and so on—making their reports as appealing as possible.

Conclusion

The activities outlined in this chapter are intended to show how cultivating students' imaginative and ecological engagement with the natural world can support them in learning to read and write. More often than not, literacy is considered an indoor activity rather than a development of a much older practice that occurs in all places and times. Long before human beings began to read the written word and use alphabetic literacy to make sense of their experiences, they survived through astute readings of the many patterns, signs, and symbols in the natural world around them.

Chapter 7 continues the discussion of this literacy unit, outlining activities that support the story forms and narrative structures discussed here. These take place in a riverside, a wood, and a riverbed.

CHAPTER 7

SITE-SPECIFIC TRACKING AND LITERACY ACTIVITIES

The activities outlined in this chapter focus on the development of both tracking and literacy skills. They are designed to support and illuminate the story or narrative formats described in chapter 6. What is different about them is that they are "site specific"—the activities were inspired by three different places: a riverside, a wooded area, and a riverbed. Some activities even evoke an "imagined place." These imagined places are often narrative contexts into which educators can embed further teaching. They often contain multiple cognitive tools that can engage students with place and with particular features of literacy.

Each activity is labelled Tracking I, Tracking II, or Tracking I and II.

- Tracking I activities are designed for primary and early elementary students (beginning and new readers), and mostly employ cognitive tools of mythic understanding.
- Tracking II activities are most suitable for engaging middle and secondary students, and mostly employ cognitive tools of romantic understanding.
- Many of the activities are suitable for all ages of students and can be easily adapted—these are the Tracking I and II activities.

Following each activity you will find a list of the kinds of literacy skills that the activity can develop; most of the lists also include suggestions for specific literacy activities.

The chapter closes with general suggestions for concluding the literacy unit and includes some specific K–Grade 2/3 and Grade 3–7 activities.

While the activities were inspired by specific riverside, wooded, and riverbed sites, they may be adapted and used in other, similar, locations. My hope is that they indicate the multitude of ways to allow cognitive tools to shape teaching and engage students with place. Ideally, your "riverside" site will have an area with sand, soil, or mud alongside the river for children to gather.

As with all outdoor learning activities, proper precautions must be taken to ensure the safety of all children. Ensure appropriate supervision at all times. When by water—and especially when engaging primary students—it would be wise to provide each child with a personal floatation device. For a more enjoyable time, students should always be dressed for the weather!

Note: In the following activities, suggestions for what you might say to students appear in *italic* text.

Site 1: Riverside

Learning to Spell—*Casting* a Spell

Tracking I and II

We don't often stop to think about the interesting double meaning of the word "spell." Use it in the context of school and students might very well groan; listening to a witch or wizard utter the word might bring a different kind of discomfort. Abram points to the magic of written letters:

> As the roman alphabet spread through oral Europe, the Old English word "spell," which had meant simply to recite a story or tale, took on the new double meaning: on the one hand, it now meant to arrange, in the proper order, the written letters that constitute the name of a thing or a person; on the other, it signified a magic formula or charm.... to assemble the letters that make up the name of a thing, in the correct order, was precisely to effect magic, to establish a new kind of influence over that entity, to summon it forth! To spell, to correctly arrange the letters to form a name or a phrase, seemed thus at the same time to *cast a spell,* to exert a new and lasting power over the things spelled.[1]

So, spelling a word with letters was magic. (The point is, of course, that it still is magic if teachers can bring students' attention to this aspect of literacy that is often taken for granted.)

Ask students to use sticks to write letter shapes in the sand or soil and, while they are doing so, to think about how the writing of letters in a certain order does indeed summon forth objects, ideas, and images. *What can you summon forth in this place at this time? (A mystical dragon? A faraway friend?)*

Abram also notes that the ability to spell—to cast a spell through the use of written letters—also influences the person who casts the spell. That is to say, when we are able to spell—read and write with alphabetic literacy—we cast a spell upon our own senses: We "exchange the wild and multiplicitous magic of an intelligent natural world for the more concentrated and refined magic of the written word."[2]

Ask students what mental images are evoked in their minds when they see the word "tree." How would they describe these images? What kinds of trees are they envisioning? Next ask them to consider at what point they "see" a tree as they read the word "tree"—is it when two, three, or all four letters combine? Next, take the students to some actual trees. Encourage them to employ their senses in encountering (hugging?) the trees. Both experiences evoke images in the mind. Both evoke our emotions. Ask students to discuss how the experiences are different.

Students can be encouraged to cast their own spells by "making tracks" in sand or soil. They can use different sticks or rocks to draw various shapes. You can then ask them to make footprints and handprints in the sand or soil. They can note different aspects of these tracks such as depth, pattern, and differences created by the sand or the soil.

Next you might encourage students to imagine a mystical animal. What being can they evoke, in this space, by creating a track? *What does this animal look like? How big is it? What does it eat? Where does it live? How does this animal move?* Each student can design the track that the foot (or hand, hoof, claw, or paw) of their imagined being would make in the ground. What spell has brought their mystical and fantastical being into this space? As a group, students can create a class set of tracks and then each child can orally evoke images of their imagined creatures.

LITERACY ACTIVITIES

★ Write letter shapes, in both upper and lower case.

★ Pair letter shapes with sounds—write letters and draw pictures of things that contain these letters or letter combinations.

★ Write different forms of punctuation.

★ Write words of differing complexity.

★ Use oral language or guided writing to describe an imaginary animal (e.g., use words that start with the letters of the alphabet or contain all the letters from A to Z).

★ Describe a place based on what students have observed and collected in the place (e.g., begin a "place" dictionary, a collection of words with corresponding sketches from A to Z; alternatively, use each letter of the alphabet and pair it with an image, sketch, or photograph).

★ Collect words or expressions that have double meanings.

- ★ Discuss how our engagement with the world changes when we employ written language; compare and contrast oral and written forms of language.

- ★ Demonstrate advanced use of verbs and engagement of metaphor (e.g., identify action words that describe what various animals or plants do—*What do trees do? Root? Sway? Branch?*).

Finding and Keeping Track (of Tracks!)

Tracking I

Students can look for signs of animal life in the sand or soil (visual signs such as tracks, other markings, paths, nests, chewed branches nearby). Students can listen for signs of animal life (audible signs such as calls or other sounds).

Whose track is it anyway? Each track tells a story. Students can work together to look for signs of animal life along the river, sketch the track in their field journals, try to identify the animal, and think about what "story" the signs or tracks tell (who, what, where, when, how?). Students can write a collaborative story based on their discoveries. Students can then find and follow their own tracks. How do they know these tracks are theirs? What is distinctive about them?

Students in this and other activities are "keeping track" of their discoveries in their journals. Ask students to think about how someone "keeps track" of the habits and movements of animals if he or she does not write these down. Encourage students to imagine that they live in a tribe where there is no written form of language. They are elders in charge of teaching the young. *How might the elders pass on their knowledge? What can they do to make the stories memorable?*

Tracking II

Students can classify tracks based on characteristics that include shape, gait, stride, and pattern. (For example, the gait reveals the shape of the animal's body. A fox has a narrow body and can put its feet in a straight line while dogs with wider bodies may have more parallel footprints. The pattern and depth of the track tells us how quickly the animal was moving. Deep, incomplete, widely spaced, or bounding patterns may indicate that the animal was running.)

Students can identify signs other than typical prints such as chew marks, homes, trails, and so on. They can record these in their tracking journals, noting signs found throughout the seasons. You might encourage them to take photos and sketches of the signs to help contribute to a track library at the school.

Students can learn a stalking walk or "fox walk" and practise moving quietly during a running game called "camouflage" (see game description on page 100). Through this game they learn about colour change as an adaptation and a useful tool when tracking.

Over time students will learn how to assess the direction of tracks and tell roughly how old they are. They can use problem-solving skills to interpret "track mysteries"— real ones and those created by you (the teacher)—learning to read the larger story using the tracks as clues. For example, FBI (Forest Bureau of Investigation) agents might come to the park and ask students for their help in tracking down who killed Sam the Sitka Spruce. Students can survey the crime scene, interview various suspects (e.g., a woodpecker, a forester) and test the soil pH, moisture, and light levels to reach a hypothesis. You can encourage older students to find/create their own tracking mysteries for other students to solve.

LITERACY ACTIVITIES

★ Use basic sight words (e.g., *saw*, *big*, *yes*) to draw, label, or describe different tracks (you can identify different words for each lesson).

★ Write names (e.g., of different animals) to continually add to a dictionary of place.

★ Describe how words and expressions can have double meanings and collect examples of these (e.g.: *Are you "keeping track" of these expressions?*).

★ Identify and use vocabulary specific to tracking (e.g., *spoor*, *quarry*, *stride*, *straddle*, *track length*, *track width*, *trailing*).

"Water, *What're* You Doing?"

Tracking I

In this activity, students play and create. They can begin by closely observing the river from various locations along the riverside. They can focus on aspects that include, for example, the river flow, textures of the riverbed, or animal life in and along the river. They can then make mini-watersheds along the riverbank and pour water along carved tunnels to see what happens. They can have float races with sticks or small constructed boats. In their journals, they can record the main features of the mini-worlds they create.

Tracking I

At riverfront, the Kanaka Creek flows smoothly by. Not quite whitewater material for an average human being. But for an ant? Now that's another story... Honey, I shrunk the kids... Principal, I shrunk the students... You might ask students to imagine what it might be like to be an ant on the river, whitewater rafting—focusing on the "riffles"—or actually living in the river on their "found" (leaf or stick) boats. Students can have boat races using their boats. *Who wins? Who loses? What kind of drama happens as the boat hits the "rapids"? Can their boats make it down the river without losing their contents?*

Tracking II

Suggest that students find a place along the riverbank to sit, observe, and imagine life on the river. Invite students to imagine what it is like, as a paddler, to come to know a river. *Paddlers watch the snow pack, the rainfall, and temperatures, and they gradually become aware of a river's moods. They come to know which rapids they can handle and what the paddling will be like at various water levels. Over time, their knowledge expands into hundreds of details, including knowing the tributaries and other rivers of the watershed. Knowing each river's personality makes them feel like old friends. To paddle a fast-flowing river you are forced to pay close attention to the subtleties of its features and currents. It requires being completely focused on the moment.*

At home or back in the classroom, encourage students to research real-life paddlers, reading the accounts of their whitewater adventures and sharing these with the class.

LITERACY ACTIVITIES

★ Practise writing and articulating vowels.

★ Describe how the body experiences vowels (e.g., Ask students to focus on the mouth and the breath as they pronounce vowels. *What does the tongue do with each vowel? How is breath released? How is the throat—open and relaxed? constricted?*).

★ Learn and use sight words (e.g., *saw, big, yes*) in oral and written formats.

★ Learn words related to water and add these to a dictionary of place.

★ Identify different individual-letter sounds and combinations of letters.

★ Identify and use alliteration (e.g.: *bubbling, babbling brook*).

★ Identify and use onomatopoeia by creating "sound words" (words with spellings that evoke actual sounds).

★ Identify homophones in language (words that sound the same but have different meanings) and use humour (e.g.: *What did the mamma frog say to the baby frog when it hurt its back? "Rub it! Rub it!"*).

★ Write about the experience of a river (e.g., from the perspective of someone boating on the river).

★ Identify and use verbs to describe the river (e.g.: *flowing, bubbling, swirling*).

★ Identify and use adjectives to describe different aspects of the river (e.g., the actual water, the flow, the river's size and shape).

Be QUIET!!

Tracking I

Students can be invited to various imagined places (the savannah, a rain forest, a jungle). With students, describe the kinds of different animals that live in a place, how they move, and their participation in a daily game of predator-prey. For example, bring students imaginatively onto the savannah. Help them to imagine the tall grass at dusk, when the female lions are coming out to hunt. *How do they move? What about their prey?* Encourage students to imaginatively "become" the gazelles, warthogs, or other creatures that live on the savannah, and imagine their movements.

Each day, teachers can bring students imaginatively along to different biomes. Everywhere on earth has spiders, bugs, creepers, or crawlers whose bodies directly affect how they move. All of these creatures have defensive and offensive strategies that keep them alive. As students enact the various locomotor and non-locomotor movements of these animals—the "animoves"—they can be engaged in a story of predator and prey in different contexts. Can students actually sneak up on someone without being heard?

Tracking II—Imagined place

Encourage students to visualize how an animal's movement is directly related to its body form. *There is a reason we do not "slither" very well as human beings.* In small groups or with a partner, have students brainstorm and list as many verbs as they can to describe how birds, insects, and animals move (e.g., by bounding, prancing, sliding, crawling, creeping). They can then think of the animals that move in each way (e.g., lions bound, snakes slither) and discuss why an animal is able to move in this way. Conclude with a contest in which students must enact each "animove"—*Who is the best slitherer? Slider? Hopper? Crawler?* Encourage students to have some fun with their observations of animals and movements—mix it up. Ask: *What would it look like if a horse were to slither or a snake to gallop? What is the weirdest possible combination of animal and movement?*

LITERACY ACTIVITIES

★ Identify words with *silent* or double letters; write/use them in sentences.

★ Create an image or story to help students remember the spelling of these special words (e.g., *climb—is that "b" the tree trunk I'm using to reach the first accessible branch?*).

★ Use adjectives to describe nouns (e.g., draw pictures of animals [the nouns] and write adjectives beside the pictures that relate to the animals' physical appearance).

- ★ Write descriptions based on observations (e.g., about an animal's nature).

- ★ Use adverbs to describe verbs (e.g., *how, exactly, do deer move? Rabbits? Bees? Wasps? What words describe their movement?*), write the adverbs (often these are words ending in *–ly*), and then invite students to move as the animals actually do.

- ★ Write simple descriptive sentences (younger students) or descriptive, informative, creative paragraphs (more advanced students) (e.g., to describe animal movement and what it's like to attempt to be very, *very* quiet).

- ★ Write a script (e.g., for a comical skit in which animals and their movements get all mixed up—*how do the animals get their own moves back?*).

- ★ Identify and use oxymorons in speech and writing (e.g., *random order, pretty ugly, original copy*). Challenge students to create their own!

Site 2: Woods

A wooded area inspired the following activities. As for the riverside activities, you can adapt these forest-based activities to suit your context. They indicate multiple ways to engage students' imaginations in learning to read and in developing a sense of place. To fully realize their aims, however, students should have access to an area with trees. A local park would be suitable or possibly some part of the school playground. Again, ensure the safety of all students with adequate supervision.

Let's Make Tracks

Tracking I and II

Ask students to create tracks in this new, wooded context. They can begin with their own footprints—can students identify each other from their footprints? Ask them to analyze the tracks: *How can we tell if footprints are moving forward or backward? How can we tell if the person making the print is running? What does the spacing between the prints indicate?* Students can then try to recreate tracks of different animals—they might be asked in advance to research an animal and be prepared to create its track for the class. Extend the activity by sending students out in pairs or small groups to find actual tracks. Ask them to analyze the tracks they find. Students might also repeat this kind of activity for different animals. Ask: *Do you know what animal it is? What clues do you have? Can you hypothesize how fast it was moving? Or how it was moving?* Students can create plaster casts of actual animal tracks. (Perhaps students want to investigate further the supposed footprints of "Big Foot"?)

★ Practise writing individual letters or combinations of letters in printed and cursive formats.

★ Identify a pattern in language and collect examples (e.g., *th* words or *ch* words).

★ Learn vocabulary specific to a topic (e.g., specific to tracking, such as names and parts of animals).

★ Write simple sentences or paragraphs (e.g., about animal movement).

★ Write riddles (e.g., that describe movement—*What animal is this?*).

★ Learn to recognize and use sight words, using analogy (e.g., each sight word indicates a different word or sound just as each track or footprint indicates a different creature).

★ Learn new words specific to a concept, using the letters of the alphabet as the first letter in each word (e.g., for the concept of the forest, woods or trees, the words "arbutus" and "arbor" for the letter *a*, and so on).

Finding and Keeping Tracks (of Tracks!) (continued)

Tracking I

Students can continue with the Finding and Keeping Tracks activity that they began in Site 1: Riverside. Students look for patterns in tracks and commonalities among tracks. They continue to collect different animal track shapes in their journals, supplementing these sketches with some details about the animals themselves. You can create prints for the students to find, identify, and compare, or students can find real ones.

Explain to students how animals move to escape predators and how we can observe changes in their movements by observing variations in their tracks.

You might create a tracking mystery for students to solve that includes a scenario such as an actual path of tracks students can follow, with a hidden "animal" at the end. *An animal is trying to escape a predator... where has it gone? How can you tell?* Encourage students to look for clues and think like animals: *Where to go? Where to hide?* Make sure students look closely at the shape, orientation or direction, depth, and so on, of the track (and at other clues about the track) to figure out where the animal might have gone. *How does the animal attempt to escape the predator? Does it move through a thickly wooded area? Does it climb a tree? How does the pattern of the tracks change along the way?*

Tracking II

Divide the class in two. Each group selects an animal and creates designs and represents or retells an adventure story about this animal. Then each group provides clues to the adventure, through the placement of tracks and other signs, for the other group of students to discover. Students can hide something at the end of their trail that the seeking students can find. The "trail detectives" need to not only find and identify the tracks and signs, but will also try to piece together the story. This activity can be repeated with students reversing roles.

You might want to play the role of a real-life trail detective (perhaps "Shadow Man" Stanley Liston of the "shadow wolves," or a skilled local hunter or elder) and share the stories of those people who are able trackers. *What are their hopes, fears, passions?*

LITERACY ACTIVITIES

★ Identify patterns in language (e.g., the capitalization of parts of a sentence, the sound and shape of verbs or adverbs).

★ Listen for common sounds created by letter combinations.

★ Identify and use rhyme, noting similarities between the sounds and spelling of rhyming words.

★ Identify and use different suffixes and prefixes.

★ Collect verbs (e.g., related to animal movement, such as hopping, sliding, galloping, slithering, crawling, creeping).

★ Write a memoir (e.g., *Memoirs of a Trail Detective*: in their journals, students can identify, sketch, and take notes about tracks and signs as they find them. They can discuss what animal they are tracking and what kinds of activities it seems the animal has been engaged in. Encourage students to carefully investigate each track, employing their increasing knowledge of what clues are given as to speed, gait, direction, etc.).

★ Write two accounts of the same story, which help students to shift perspectives (e.g., one story can be from the perspective of a trail detective and another from the perspective of the animal. *What kind of richness of detail can be added to the animal's account that the trail detective doesn't learn from tracks?*).

The Deer's View; The Photographer's View

Tracking I and II

Ask students to "act out" the following story as either the deer or the photographer. Encourage them to re-enact the events based on the imagery and feelings the following texts evoke in their minds as they hear the passages read aloud. To support their thinking—and planning—you might slowly and carefully read the text aloud several times. Suggest to students that as they listen they should take note of their feelings, of images that they have in their minds, and of particular details that come into focus.

The Deer

Early in the morning, raindrops that collected on the fir boughs yesterday are splattering on the ground. A few drops hit the fur on my back and I turn my neck to lick it dry. I pause to chew on some cedar boughs. In the distance I hear some twigs snap and I stop to look down the river. My ears swivel and I sniff the air as I wait. I smell a trace of something strange, a scent that I have yet to notice in the forest. The wind picks up and I can no longer discern the smell so I move down to the riverbank. The ground is slippery from all the rain; I spread my hooves for more grip and bend down to take a sip from the water. Again, I hear a noise, very faint this time. I freeze and turn my ears in the direction of the noise. This time it is closer. I bound away from the river to the forest's edge. I feel safe now under the shelter of the hemlocks and I bring the cedar boughs up from my first stomach to keep chewing on them. My mother has been feeding in the grove beside me and she moves closer when she sees me. Soft snow starts to fall; frost has formed on my chin and I can see the trail of my breath dance in the air. Suddenly, my mother snorts loudly and I raise my head to see a two-legged animal crouched nearby. My mother wheezes loudly and starts bounding uphill. There is a loud thrashing of twigs and branches as we dart away from this creature. I bound as quickly as I can, the greens of the forest blurring together as I leap over the logs and huckleberry bushes, keeping an eye on the black tail of my mother. The smell of fir eventually masks the sharp, sickly sweet scent of the creature. All is quiet again; I am left with the still forest and a racing heart.

The Photographer

Walking along the riverbank, I can hear the water gurgling in pockets of rock. The forest is quiet today and there is a chill to the air. I wrap my camera strap around my neck and stuff my hands into my pockets to keep them warm. On the right-hand side of the trail the grass has been flattened into three large circles—a deer bed, I suspect. Looks like a nice sheltered spot. I move closer to the bed, stepping on a few old twigs, to get a good shot. As I take the lens cap off my camera, snow begins to softly fall around me. The grass on the ground looks mint-green behind the swirling snow. I try a few angles and move on. Up ahead I spot some heart-shaped deer tracks along the muddy trail. Looking close, I can see the small hooves of a fawn or yearling. I bend down to examine them more carefully: the edges of the prints are well defined and I can tell the tracks are fresh. All four feet are close together, and I can see marks from the tiny dewclaws; it must have been running, bounding. I wonder what startled it. I follow the prints until they enter the forest and I lose track of them as the ground is covered with the sludge of decaying maple leaves. I notice though that there are some frayed edges on the twigs of a cedar sapling—the deer have been feeding here. I crouch to take a picture and a loud grunt startles me, I look up to see two deer bounding through the forest. They were right beside me and I had not noticed! I watch their chalky brown coats and black tails quickly bound through the hemlocks and falling snow, hooves crashing down on damp leaves and branches. Then all is quiet again. I am left with the still forest and a racing heart.

Extend the activity by challenging students to represent or describe the deer's experience visually. Alternatively, ask students to imagine a new scenario in which they encounter a different animal in the woods. Using the above story as a model, their task is to describe in evocative language how the human and the animal share an experience in remarkably different ways. Conclude by asking students about the limitations of this kind of activity. *Can we ever know what it is like to be in another's shoes? hooves? paws?*

LITERACY ACTIVITIES

★ Identify and employ adjectives, adverbs, verbs, and nouns (e.g., in relation to local plants, animals, and events).

★ Describe an event from different points of view (e.g., from the perspectives of different plant and animal species).

Awaken the Senses!

Tracking I and II

Like tribal hunters, student trackers need to awaken their senses:

Sight: Students can practise "splatter vision" or wide-angle vision to find a hidden object within the forest (e.g., a pencil). Encourage students to try to look both more closely and more broadly, to actually look at and seek out things in their visual field that don't initially attract their visual attention, to catch—simultaneously—multiple features of the patterned images before their eyes. Students can also observe and discuss local animals that have great sight adaptations (e.g., hawks, dragonflies, bees).

Sound: Students can learn how a larger ear surface area helps animals (e.g., deer and rabbits) to amplify noises and thus hear extremely well. Students might cup their hands behind their ears and listen to see if they can hear better. Students can do a "silent sit and sound map"—they sit silently, focusing their attention on the sounds around them. Ask them to track the noises they hear and to record how the sounds make them feel, encouraging them to be descriptive—instead of labelling a noise as a "bird" they should write the actual sound of the bird's call (e.g., *wik, wik, wik, wee*). They can sketch a map of the place on which they try to locate the sounds. *Where are the sounds coming from?*

Smell: Younger students can collect various items (no picking of living plants!) to make a delectable forest "perfume" in small cups. The aim is to focus on the olfactory sense. *What subtle and different smells can be created using found objects?* Older students can create guided scent maps or trails for a small section of the forest, imagining the space as a coyote would experience it.

Touch: Older students can help guide younger ones to search for various textures within the forest. Younger students can classify the items according to textures. Older students can be challenged to come up with explanations for why an item has a particular texture. (For example, fir cones have tough, woody scales that protect the seeds inside and slowly open when the time is right to release the seeds. Each seed is attached to a soft, feather-shaped "wing" to help it fly well on the wind.)

Taste: *Flies have the unique ability to taste with their feet. Is that truly odd or is it odd because we are accustomed to tasting with our mouths?* Students can drink tea made from fir needles or eat local berries, both rich in vitamin C. Students can try eating salmon-berries or blackberries one drupe at a time (the berry itself is a large group of drupes; each drupe is the fleshy part surrounding a small seed). Older students can research local edible plants. (Please use caution with this activity. Students need to be aware that some berries and plants are poisonous!)

Tracking II—Imagined place

Living wide awake has its benefits. In addition to learning more about the living and nonliving entities we share this place with, we realize "I" or "me" doesn't end at the skin. With our senses wide awake and the skill to read the messages in nature, we can come to see how we are implicated in the lives of the animals we study. We are part of nature.

Ask students to imagine they have jumped into the pages of a magical book. They must figure out where they are and who or what might be watching them. They will need to use their senses and knowledge of tracking to find clues to where they are. *What is this place? Where is this place? Who lives here?* To begin this activity, you can read the following text.

> Okay, it's time to "wake up" your awareness. Close your eyes. I'd like you to imagine you are at a library. You can smell that musty, somewhat sickly smell of books. Fluorescent lights make the room stark, uninviting. Your sneakers are wet. They squeak on the tiled floor of the entryway. You squeak your way upstairs to find something to read. On the second floor of the library you encounter shelves upon shelves of books. Where to start? Where to look? You don't really know what you feel like reading. You don't have anything particular in mind.
>
> Somewhat overwhelmed, you notice a book lying out on a table in an area designated for reading and studying. You are drawn to the gold lettering on the spine of the book. You read the words "Come here." The gold lettering shines off the cover of the book, illuminated somehow. The title on the front puzzles you… against a backdrop of what appear to be interconnected branches and vines, it says "Open Me." Odd. You can't help but open the book to the first page. You begin to read. As you do so, you enter the world in the words. You are transported into a forest.

OPEN YOUR EYES. Where are you? Your challenge: Remain wide awake. Let the place wash over you. Identify where you are. Look for signs of who and what shares the place with you.

LITERACY ACTIVITIES

★ Collect or organize "new" language that describes more acutely different forms of sensory engagement or objects (e.g., *drupe*).

★ Draw and label a picture (e.g., of what the forest looks like when someone's senses are wide awake).

★ Use traditional forms of punctuation to express feelings. Invent new punctuation marks that can help express emotions and experiences.

★ Use the body to demonstrate the functions of different forms of punctuation (e.g., use gesture or sound to indicate the purpose of a period or a semi-colon).

★ Design and write a book cover (e.g., students might design the cover of a magical book that "calls them to dive into" an imagined place or write about their adventure in an imagined place).

Tree Story

Tracking I

Take students out to a place where there are two different kinds of trees (e.g., a spruce and a cottonwood). Encourage them to closely examine the trees. *How are these trees different in appearance?* Students can create leaf and bark rubbings using found materials from these different kinds of trees. Engage students in identifying different stages of tree growth. Students can look for examples of trees in the forest that are at different stages of growth, from seed to sapling to giant tower. *What words best describe these stages?* How might students use their bodies to represent the growth of a tree from small seed to decaying log?

What does a tree need to grow? Students can make "forest soup" and then feed a tree of their choice. In small bowls, students can collect all the materials trees need to grow. (The recipe: add some soil, leaves, sticks, and rocks for nutrients, blow on it for air, hold it up to the sky for sun, and add water.) Choose a tree to feed the soup to and say, "Bon Appétit!"

What is it like to be a tree? Have students practise the "tree" and other yoga postures as a way to take on alternative perspectives. (Review the poses described in chapter 4.) You might guide them through the posture and through mental imagery to feel the strength and permanence of the tree. *When someone looks at a tree, there are certain features that are immediately obvious: trunk, branches, leaves, or perhaps the crown or bark.* If you encourage students to pause and think about the qualities that a tree represents, it may evoke a different, deeper, understanding. Doing the tree pose may lead into a discussion of qualities that include, for example, uprightness, rootedness, strength, and even alignment. As students practise the tree pose, guide and encourage them to breathe deeply, asking them to be mindful of their bodies. *How, like a tree, do you feel the air around you? Do you feel wind? How do you interact with the wind without losing your balance? Are you firmly rooted? Do you feel strong or vulnerable in the pose?*

Tracking II

Students can create a table to compare the physical features of two (or more) types of tree. Have them list the main parts of a tree in the first column (e.g., roots, trunk, branches, leaves), and the different tree types they are going to compare in the first row (e.g., cottonwood, spruce). They can then write words in the table cells, describing different parts of each tree. *Do the same adjectives apply to each type of tree?* Students can then think about what the trees are actively *doing,* and add a third column for verbs that describe each tree (e.g., branching, balancing, swaying, rooting, cleaning, housing, dancing). In creating these lists, students could also learn about the vital part trees and other plants play in cleaning the air.

Students can write some fiction or non-fiction about the forest and its trees as they learn more about the form and function of particular trees. *What's the story on this tree? What has it observed? What does it feel? What animals call it home? What creatures have walked across its trunk or burrowed into its bark? What creatures have swung on its branches?* Students can share their stories by acting out "conversations" between two types of trees. *What does each provide the other in this environment? How do they compete for survival? How do they enable each other's survival? Which is the biggest? In the scheme of trees, what species really is the biggest and how many times bigger is one of these tree giants than, for example, a spruce or cottonwood?*

LITERACY ACTIVITIES

★ Demonstrate basic reading comprehension (e.g., Read a short fiction story about trees and talk about what happened in the story, read non-fiction about trees and have students incorporate their understanding into the tree information they have in their journals, or create a story orally as a class with each student adding a sentence. Students can also create written stories as a class, using the same process, and then edit and correct each other's writing; when they are finished they can practise reading the story to others at school or at home).

★ Have students write their own stories (e.g., to help identify different tree forms; you might read *A Special Gift* by Andrea Spalding: *What's the special gift?* As indicated in this story, you can identify the Douglas fir cone by the little "mouse" that appears to be inside it. If you look between the scales of a cone, it looks like the back legs and tail of a little mouse are sticking out).

* Write words as labels (e.g., draw a tree and label the different parts of it).

* Use imagery to learn grammar (e.g., compare "parts of a tree" to "parts of a sentence." *What are the main features of a sentence?*).

* Use vocabulary to create word pictures (e.g., words about trees that are written in the shape of a tree).

Branching Out

Tracking I

Students can focus their attention on different types of branches and their characteristics. Using digital photography and sketching in their field journals, as well as taking detailed notes, students can collect information on different aspects of branches, including shape, size, bark, leaves, and so on. They can keep different lists and be encouraged to organize these. *What living things can you observe on the branches you investigate? Did you find any nests? If so, can you notice any patterns as to where the nests are located? For example, oriole nests are often near the tip of a branch; robin nests are often in the nook where the branch meets the trunk of the tree. Why do the birds locate their nests in different places on the branch?*

Students can take a different perspective on trees, for example: a slug's view by lying on their backs on the forest floor, beneath the branches, and looking up through the canopy. *What do the branches give to the forest floor? Why do the branches grow as they do? Where does the understory begin? The canopy influences plant growth—what do you notice? For example, some plants and trees are in the shade (e.g., hemlock trees and ferns) while others are in the sun (e.g., alder trees).* Students can also consider "branching" patterns in places other than the forest canopy. *What about the veins in a leaf? How about the patterns made by the lines on the back of the hand?* Ask students, still viewing the forest from a slug's perspective, to look for tracks above their heads. *What evidence of animals can you see in the foliage around you? What animals can be tracked (e.g., visually, audibly)?*

Tracking II

Ask students to "collect" tree skeletons they see when they take a slug's point of view. First they can draw the branching patterns of various trees, and then they can choose a tree and develop a hypothesis as to why its branches are shaped as they are (e.g., a big-leaf maple tree maximizes the surface area facing the sun; a spruce's sloped, flexible branches prevent snow from accumulating and branches from breaking). Imagining themselves as scientists (*a magical potion quickly turns our slugs into scientists—available at most pharmacies by prescription*), students can report on various adaptations of trees (e.g., of the branches, bark, and leaves) to their environments.

Trees are often hosts for other plants. Students can look for epiphytes (plants that grow on other plants but are not parasitic; a fern is an example of an epiphyte). Students might marvel at how some epiphytes survive, such as the ones that tower far over the forest floor without the need for soil. *How many different examples can you find?* Epiphytes are highly diverse; you can expect to find somewhere between 40 to 70 species in an acre of forest! Students can research extreme examples of epiphytes, comparing those present in a particular place with the monstrous epiphytes found in a tropical rainforest or other ecosystem. Tell students the stories of real-life botanists who study epiphytes or who are epiphyte collectors. *What are their stories? Who first named or identified epiphytes? What we re or are their hopes, fears, or passions?*

LITERACY ACTIVITIES

★ Use metaphor (e.g., identify forest-related metaphors such as *taking root* and *branching out,* or create or add to a list of examples of metaphors; encourage students to write new examples down as they hear them; discuss examples as they are noted: *If someone is "branching out," what does that mean? Why do we call a sheet of paper in a book a leaf? Does anyone have a canopy on their bed?*).

★ Use different grammatical tenses—past, present, future—to describe the life story of a tree. Draw a tree shape and use it to categorize features of language (e.g., draw a tree trunk with branches for nouns, verbs, adverbs, adjectives, homophones, synonyms, antonyms, etc.). Students can write examples of each kind of word—words that are related to their forest studies—on each branch.

★ Find and write antonyms (look for, draw, and label opposites they find in the forest).

★ Share, orally or in print, the story of the understory (e.g.: *What are the survival stories of living things in this area? When sunlight is in high demand, what kinds of strategies enable plants to survive?* Students can write an informational or expository text, such as "Survival Strategies in the Understory").

Bird Watching

Tracking I and II

Students can focus specifically on local birds by looking for, sketching, and comparing the tracks of various birds they find in the soil or sand. (You might want to "plant" a few prints ahead of time.) *How do the feet of a crow differ from those of a goose? What do these kinds of birds look like and sound like? Can you hear these birds? Where do they nest?* Next to the bird tracks they've drawn in their field journals, students can begin to collect information about the appearance of different birds. *How big are the birds? What colour are they? What are their feathers like? Can anyone find a feather? What do the birds' droppings look like?* Students can also collect information about birds' feeding and nesting habits, and calls. *Are we being watched by these birds right now? Identifying bird calls is one of the best ways to know if you're being watched.* You can encourage students to learn bird language—they can practise making and listening to bird calls and songs. *Of course, it can be hard at times to identify birds from their calls—what other clues might help us tell birds apart?*

LITERACY ACTIVITIES

★ Collect specific vocabulary words and language (e.g., words and language related to birds: *What does it mean to say that "birds of a feather flock together"? My brother just told me I had a "bird brain." Is this a good thing? I wouldn't mind having "hawk vision," but a "bird brain"?*).

★ Spell phonetically, to demonstrate students' understanding of different letter sounds and their combinations (e.g., spell the bird calls they are learning to identify).

★ Identify and use homophones, and discuss the language clues that can help us tell them apart. Personalize homophones (e.g., *What would Mr. Meat be like—always hungry? —versus Mr. Meet—super-chatty? —or Mr. Mete—always telling people off?*; then draw a sketch to differentiate the words.

★ Identify and use the superlative—write about the "bests" and "worsts" by indicating in what ways birds, or other animals or plants, are extraordinary (e.g., a hawk has extremely good vision—*a hawkeye*). Rank birds: *smallest, lightest, brightest, largest, loudest call, highest-pitch call, fastest-tempo call,* and so on.

★ Identify the unique skills and qualities of animals (e.g., each of a deer's eyes has 310° vision, and a deer also has an acute sense of smell and can detect predators from a long distance; a fawn will begin to walk about 20 minutes after birth; if you thought your hair or nails grew quickly, think again—the tissue in deer antlers is the fastest-growing living tissue on earth; one more—I can't help it: deer have hollow hair that insulates them and keeps them from drowning). Students can use the superlative structure to express the amazing animal facts they discover in their research.

Stalking

Tracking I and II

This is an activity all teachers will love: students have to be as quiet as possible. Before you ask students to be quiet in games and other physical activities, guide them through some breathing and stillness activities and have them reflect on what it *feels* like to be quiet. Younger students can use individual words and older ones can use more detailed writing, from their journals, to think about the following: *What does "quiet" feel like in the body? What does "quiet" look like? (It's not necessarily being still.)* You can ask your students to run a certain distance without them attempting to be quiet at all, and then do the same thing without making a sound. They can then reflect on what they had to think about when quietness was a goal.

Have students practise moving through the forest as quietly as possible. Then "test" them in a game where students who are heard by their peers or the teacher get eliminated. There are lots of games that rely on children (of all ages) being quiet. Some of these are:

- **Camouflage:** One student is the predator animal and the rest of the students are prey. The predator stays in one spot and allows the prey to hide (while counting up to 10 or so). The predator then opens her eyes and describes the clothing of anyone she sees hiding. For example, the predator might say, *"I see blue jeans and a red shirt."* Students who hear their clothing being described are "found" and must reveal themselves and return to the starting place. When the predator can no longer spot anyone, students can switch roles and a new predator can be selected. The game can also be modified: for example, the prey must hide, stay still, and close their eyes. The new predator moves about and will try to tag the prey without being heard. If any of the prey hears a predator, they point in the direction of the sound and the predator is out.

- **Sleeping miser:** One student—the "sleeping miser"—sits in the middle of a circle of students, blindfolded, with some keys on the floor in front of him. The students in the circle take turns trying to take the keys quietly. To be proclaimed the winner, a student must take the keys and sit down without the "sleeping miser" noticing. The sleeping miser points in the direction that he hears a noise. If the person "stalking" the keys is pointed at, he must sit down.

- **Rabbit ears:** A student takes the role of the prey and moves away from the others with her back turned to the group. The rest of the group (the predators) has to quietly sneak up on the prey. If the prey hears a noise, she turns around and the predators must freeze. Anyone who is seen moving has to go back to a starting point. The game ends when one of the predators tags the prey.

- **Animal tag:** Each student in the group is assigned a different animal from within the food chain. Herbivores collect tokens from stations that the teacher has set up ahead of time. The challenge is for herbivores to collect tokens without being tagged by predators. If a herbivore is tagged, he must give up a certain number of tokens, depending on his level in the food chain. The animal with the most tokens at the end wins. Different elements can change the difficulty level; for example, tokens can be lost for natural or human interference in the animal habitat or you can declare "Drought!" in the middle of the game, at which point all the players in a certain area (the drought area) must give back a token, or two. You decide. Another example: A forest fire might result in all the players having to give back all the tokens they've collected.

★ Develop expository writing (e.g., write a "how to" book for stalking).

★ Develop a set of written or oral rules (e.g., create and lead a game that relies on being quiet).

Site 3: Riverbed

The riverbed area that inspired the following activities is a largely rocky area that is submersed for parts of the year. When it is not, however, it offers pools of water and, on the bed and banks, great evidence of the past. Adapt these activities as needed, even to a riverbank if that is all you can access. Be sure to take safety precautions, as always, with these outdoor activities.

Making a Good Impression—Evidence of the Past

Tracking I and II

If we are skilled enough, we can also read signs of things that happened long ago. Introduce students to fossils, perhaps using the text provided below, which gives students an idea of the immense time scale of fossils. *A fossil is a really, REALLY good impression. Fossils are incredibly old.* To students who think their teacher is ancient, an age of 40 to 50 million years is off the charts. In order to evoke students' sense of wonder, think about how to illustrate just how long ago that was. Age is one emotionally engaging thing about fossils. What is possibly more magical about fossils is that they are incredibly rare.

Most of life is worn away in the river of time leaving not a trace behind. Very, very rarely, in strange circumstances, some individual life forms are preserved. From these we glimpse the incredible variety of creatures that have lived here before us. Without fossils, we would have no idea about any of these creatures, nor would we have been able to work out the story of evolution. You might try to give students a sense of how fossils (these accidental remnants) are our key to lost worlds.

Show students real fossils or images of fossils and ask them to brainstorm what they can tell just by looking at each fossil or picture. Ideally, show the students images of fossils from your area and describe them. For example, imagine the particular fossil being described here: *This image of a fossil shows four leaves parallel to one another. The leaves were caught in the current at the time and so the fossil is not only a track of the plant that once existed but of the water and its direction. This fossil tells a story—it is a snapshot in time.*

Students can use plaster to make their own fossils, capturing prints of leaves or other natural objects. Once these are made, the students can imagine it is thousands of years in the future and their fossil has been found. *What will scientists say about it?*

Students can be enlisted as detectives looking for some indicators of what the local area was like in the past. *What other clues can tell us about the past here?* Possible answers include the following:

- The shape of a river or riverbed indicate an area's past geological features.
- The features of the rock in the riverbed indicate characteristics of the past rock or soil in the area. *What debris has run or now runs in the river water? What may have eroded or now erodes the rock? What kind of rock is present? Can layers be seen?*
- The size and width of tree rings indicate something about past growing conditions.

Students can examine the layers of rock along the riverbank. *What do the layers tell us? What accounts for different thickness?* Guide them in imagining the kind of pressure and time required to create the rock. *What does it feel like to be "under pressure"?* The point of this discussion would be to indicate the effect of time on place and that we can be time detectives and get a glimpse about past conditions through evidence that is around us. But truly, what our contexts looked like millions of years ago is a big mystery that no one can know with any certainty. Most likely it was a swampy river delta. *What kinds of animals—and of what immense size—roamed this land?* Students can draw a picture of what they imagine the place they live in looked like at the time in which the item in the fossil you showed them was actually a living thing (in the previous example, the fossil is a leaf).

LITERACY ACTIVITIES

★ Identify and use different tenses (past, present, future) and moods (indicative, subjunctive, conditional).

★ Compare how written language is used to express what will happen (the future), what is happening (the present), and what has happened (the past). (For example: Identify some of the patterns, such as *-ed* in the past tense for some verbs. *What are exceptions to this?* Evoke wonder at what verb tenses actually do—they transport us in time! *We mustn't forget that the past tense is a human creation. Someone, somewhere, invented it.*)

★ Write short stories (e.g., describe the "lost" worlds captured in fossils).

★ Use description (e.g., describe how the written word is like a "fossil"; using the previous example, ask students: *How are the four leaves cast in the fossil from this place different from the plant itself? What is lost? What does the fossil preserve? What is revealed? What is concealed? In comparison, how are spoken words different from written words? What is lost? What is gained? Do the gains of literacy come at a cost?*).

★ Identify and use the superlative (e.g., research and write about record-breaking fossils—the biggest, most shocking ones found. *Where? When? By whom? What's the story?*).

★ Investigate a real archaeologist (e.g., research and document his or her accomplishments, interests, passions, hopes, and fears, and then role-play this person; come to school "in role" to meet other great scientists for a "dig" at their location; throughout the day students can present themselves in role, sharing their various levels of expertise, taking note of new discoveries, and eventually writing a final report).

★ Write biographical texts (e.g., *About Me*; students can describe what they are like at this moment: their likes, dislikes, hopes, fears, passions, etc.; they can write words to describe themselves—"me" poems, perhaps—along the shape of a traced hand or foot; they can use plaster to capture a handprint or foot-print; their prints might reveal how they lived, but what additional details reveal what they are like?).

★ Identify and use metaphor (e.g.: *Making a good impression; My grandpa is a fossil*).

★ Identify and use compound words (e.g., sandstone: *What's the story on sand-stone?* Encourage students to investigate how sandstone is formed; identify the story behind other compound words, such as workhorse, sweetheart, footlocker).

★ Collect sketches of patterning on rocks (e.g.: *What name can you give each pattern? Imagine this pattern is the next big style in vinyl or wallpaper.* Students can write words about rocks in a field journal; note differences in colour, pattern, texture. *How do river rocks and pebbles compare to shale or sandstone?*).

Life in the Water

Tracking I and II

Students can turn their attention to the water pools in the riverbed. Imagining they are scientists, students can begin by closely observing what they see below the surface of the water. They must document their findings. *How many different things do you observe?* The aim is to somehow organize their findings. They might start with living or non-living as a preliminary organizational tool. *How do you know if the objects you see are alive or dead?* They may not always be sure if something is living or dead; these items can be carefully described for discussion with their peers. Students might need to refine their organiza-tion. They can look at each category and see what additional subdivision they might make to categorize what they find in the water. *Did anyone, for example, find any invertebrates under rocks in the river pools?*

Encourage students to experiment with floating objects in the riverbed pools. Using objects they collect from the immediate vicinity, students can try to identify the principles that make some things float and other things sink. *What's the secret to floating?*

Why not take a fish-eye view of the water? Have students kneel down over shallow pools of water in the riverbed, wearing snorkelling masks, and put their faces in the water. Ask them to write two different sets of impressions: life in the water from the perspective of a land animal and life in the water from the perspective of a fish. Two sets of adjectives may be used to describe the water. *What adjectives are used for both? What kind of new understanding do you gain from partial immersion?*

LITERACY ACTIVITIES

★ Write short pieces that focus on perspective (e.g., describing what it might be like to live in water; students can think about being underwater themselves, as swimmers, but they can also be encouraged to choose one living organism from a pool in a riverbed and imagine, from that creature's perspective, what water life is like; depending on the organism they choose, they can articulate the kinds of sensations that water life brings and the kinds of images that might be "seen," etc.).

★ Write creative paragraphs (e.g., describing, from the perspective of a chosen creature from a pool in a riverbed, what it was like the day its life changed, that is, the day it was taken from its water home by a human hand—the student's hand—and held in the air, touched, poked, and perhaps laid on a rock surface; you can adapt "free write" activities to meet students' literacy levels and needs—e.g., the newest readers might simply identify and write key words describing what the adventure would be like, but older students will, of course, be able to write more freely).

Rock On! Of Rocks and Living Things

Tracking I

Depending on the time of year—and, thus, the water level—students can spend a day walking upstream. Their task will be to track the changes they observe in relation to one of the following features of place: the riverbed, the riverside, rock formation, water collections, life forms, and surrounding foliage. With the data they collect as a class, they can compare different places in the riverbed in terms of tracking time. *Where are the best indicators of the past? What are these clues? Why here?* They can identify patterns in the landscape and use these as a basis for some written reflections on the stories these patterns tell. You can encourage them to think of each "clue" of time's passing or each pattern as something wonderful and mysterious. You might read the following poem by William Blake and ask them what thoughts and images the poem evokes.

To see a world in a grain of sand
and a heaven in a wild flower,
Hold infinity in the palm of your hand,
And eternity in an hour.[3]

What kind of wonder do you see? You might give students time to do a "free write" response to the poem, and share it in pairs and with the whole class.

Tracking II

Students can develop a series of maps of various geological and/or biological dimensions of the area. Young students can map particular geographical features of the place in rudimentary maps. Older students can either create an entire map or use pre-existing black-and-white topographical or trail maps as the basis for making their own maps. To focus on geology, as students explore the area, they can take notes on the map of what kind of rocks are below their feet or around them. They can use coloured pencils to classify and colour on the map the different kinds of rocks. To focus on biology, students can do the same kind of exploration but create maps indicating the forms of life they notice around them. They can classify the plant and animal life they notice in a way that they can represent on their "life" map of the area. It might be a wise idea to ask students to focus on different aspects of the flora—there is too much life to show on one map!

The map is, of course, an abstraction. Ask the students to reflect upon how a map of a place is different from the actual place. You can challenge them to think of a way to make a map that is more reflective of the richness of a place. *How would we represent our emotional attachments on a map? How can we evoke wonder on a map?*

Students can practise using maps. You might give them trail maps and ask them to follow the maps. Everyone loves a good treasure hunt—you might prepare a treasure hunt with maps and clues, or your students could work in groups to prepare treasure hunts for their peers.

LITERACY ACTIVITIES

★ Make a list (e.g., of changes students observe as they walk upstream).

★ Use correct terminology (e.g., in labelling maps).

★ Design a map (e.g., a map that shows emotional engagement; orally discuss or explain through written language how this is a "wonder" map).

★ Create a map with labels (e.g., locate changes students observe on a map and correctly label the features).

★ Discuss the relationship between a map and a place.

- ★ Write free verse poetry (e.g., based on something that surprises students or evokes their sense of wonder as they track time in the riverbed).

- ★ Write a rebus poem.

- ★ Read poetry (e.g., by William Wordsworth, or perhaps by more contemporary poets who marvel at the beauty in the natural, everyday world).

- ★ Learn about different forms of poetry (e.g., read examples of poetry and then ask students to write their own poetry, based on what inspires them in place).

- ★ Use written language to compare and contrast a map and a place (e.g., a Venn diagram).

My Name, My Call: Come Find Me!

Tracking I and II

Students have human names that identify them. They use their voices in ways that connect them to others in their community. Students can develop their auditory skills by creating a distinctive sound or "call" that they can use to identify themselves. They can use these calls as the basis of various tracking games. For example, once they have made up their own sounds, students can hide somewhere and their peers can find them based solely on the sounds they make.

Encourage students to track to their source the natural calls or sounds they hear. *Did you hear that sound? What was that? Where did it come from? How do you know? If you hear branches rustling, what's the cause? If you hear a ripple in the water, can you find the rock?*

LITERACY ACTIVITIES

- ★ Make journal entries (e.g., describing students' calls and why they chose them).

- ★ Employ multiple literacy strategies within an imaginative context (e.g., Imagine a day in a local park or natural area when everyone hears a sound they cannot identify. [You can make this happen.] *What is making the sound?* Find clues of what might be making the sound. *Are there tracks? Other evidence?* [You can make this happen too!]. Using the information learned from the sound—possibly the location or the direction—and the tracks discovered, describe the mystical creature that is making the sound. *What kind of body does it have? How is the sound being made? How does the animal move? When does it make the sound? What is it trying to communicate with this sound?*).

Soundscapes

Tracking I and II

This activity builds on R. Murray Schafer's concept of the "soundscape."[4] It brings together the kinds of auditory observations students have been making about place. Schafer defines a soundscape as the sound or combination of sounds that forms or arises from an immersive environment. The soundscape refers to both the natural acoustic environment (natural sounds, including animal vocalizations, sounds of weather, and other natural elements) and human sounds (including ordinary human activities such as conversation, songs and music, sounds of work, and sounds of mechanical origin or industrial activity). In a park, the soundscape is created largely from the natural acoustic environment, but also has elements from the human environment.

Sounds of the riverbed inspired this activity for me, but the activity could be adapted to any of the three areas (riverside, woods, riverbed). You can ask students what different soundscapes they can identify; what they demonstrate will indicate their growing awareness of the uniqueness of different places.

Discuss with students the three aspects of soundscape: *keynote sounds, sound signals* (also referred to as a figure sounds), and *soundmarks*. A keynote is a musical term that identifies the key of a piece of music. In nature, it is the basic environmental sound that is always there, but humans are not always conscious of it. The keynote sound can be created from natural sources (e.g., by animals, geography, and climate) or human activity (e.g., traffic). A sound signal is a foreground sound that humans consciously notice (e.g., bells, whistles, horns, sirens, and so on). These sound signals can be surprising, sudden, or possibly annoying. A soundmark is the auditory equivalent of a landmark; it is a sound that is unique to an area and that people consciously identify with a particular place. Soundmarks can originate from many human and natural sources. They include the call of a local bird species, the ringing of bells in a local clock tower, the sound of a train's whistle, or the acoustics stemming from local tourist attractions, such as the dramatic rushing sound of a specific amusement park ride.

Students can listen for these three aspects of soundscapes in an area. Encourage students to be quiet and reflective. *Can you identify the aspects of a soundscape and describe them? How does each type of sound make you feel?*

Students can record the soundscapes of different areas and in different places in the community, and play these back, comparing and contrasting the various soundscapes. *What kinds of feelings are evoked as you hear these soundscapes?* Can students identify where different places are from their soundmarks?

LITERACY ACTIVITIES

★ Write sounds phonetically (e.g., *Think about the range of sounds human beings can make with their bodies. Can all the sounds we make be written phonetically? How is the body used differently to create the sounds of languages around the world?*).

★ Identify and use onomatopoeia (e.g., by listening to place sounds and then writing words to recreate these sounds).

A Few Concluding Activities

This literacy unit should be concluded in a way that allows students to bring the story form/narrative of tracking and reading to a celebratory closure. As students have learned to track, the invisible has become visible. The meaningless marks in the sand and the squiggles on a page have become meaningful. Learning to decipher the tracks of animals has enhanced students' awareness of the living world around them. Their ability to identify letters, sounds, and words has expanded their sense of the world around them.

How can students' new skills and knowledge be integrated into activities that connect literacy and place and, more importantly, allow students opportunities to make the knowledge their own? What kinds of activities can showcase students' growing literacy skills *and* their sense of place?

You could, of course, conclude this unit with activities that emphasize basic literacy skills and that align with established evaluation and grading practices. You are likely very familiar with a range of formative and summative activities students can complete in order to demonstrate specific literacy skills, so I will not review these traditional activities. Instead, the activities that follow are examples of ways in which imaginative and ecological educators can provide opportunities for students to express both their literacy skills and their growing sense of place and its inhabitants. The aim is to conclude teaching units with activities that allow students to demonstrate their knowledge of place and their developing emotional connections with it, as well as the nature of their imaginative engagement in the unit.

Place-based Activities for Primary and Elementary Students

Creative writing

Students can do some creative writing that is inspired by place. The youngest students could add this writing to their dictionary of place (the collection of words and images from A to Z that they started in the Learning to Spell activity, pages 83–85), inspired by the places they have engaged with over the course of the unit.

Place poems

Students can compose a collection of place poems in which they use their vocabulary about place to describe their favourite or special places. Poems could be rhyming and playful, or free verse. The aim is to create a detailed and intimate description of each child's experience with some particular aspects of place, using vivid imagery.

"My Place" project

To connect more intimately to their personal experiences, students can create a "my place" project, reflecting what they found most emotionally and imaginatively engaging in each of the three sites (riverside, woods, riverbed). The project could be a children's book, or a series of postcards where students pair an image of a specific place with a short text describing what they found wonderful about it.

Place-based Activities for Middle and Secondary Students

Tracking library

Students can compile a tracking library—a collection of photos, drawings, and journal entries detailing the different tracks they found throughout the unit that reflect their learning. The tracking library collections could be kept for use by students in subsequent years.

Tracking guides

Students can create guides to tracking that indicate how a tourist or someone new to a place might learn about the inhabitants of the forest, the diversity of fauna, and the history of the place.

Songlines

Students can create their own songlines—poetic representations of place that imaginatively map the place. In some oral language–based cultures (particularly among Aboriginal peoples of Australia), songlines represent the tracks of their ancestors across the land. By creating a songline, students represent the place through language and music, creating an auditory map that someone can follow to navigate the place. The melody and tone of the music depict the varying terrain and evoke how students imaginatively and emotionally engaged with place. In this final activity, students can sing back to the land a response to their engagement with place.

CHAPTER 8

DEVELOPING AND SUSTAINING AN
IEE PROGRAM

From about three years of age, Chloë has been fascinated with dandelions. To her, they are one of the world's greatest wonders. From the explosive yellow petals of a dandelion in bloom through to the baldness of an empty seed head, she considers each one beautiful and captivating. She will often kneel amid the patches of dandelions in the local park. She carefully selects one. The whispery white seed head forms a perfect sphere. Within it exists a pattern of lines and textures she didn't notice yesterday or the day before. Her eyes are wide as she looks closer. The softness of the seed head tickles her nose just moments before the long, slow breath that propels the tiny seed-parachutes into the air around her. As the seeds encircle her, slowly making their way towards the grass, she wonders where each will land, what each will become, how there can be so few dandelions around her compared to the number of seeds released by each one. And why, *why*, she asks, are they so fluffy and white today when yesterday they were so shockingly yellow?

We can learn a lot from observing children as they engage with the world around them. In this case, Chloë's captivation with the intricate patterns contained within the seed head of the dandelion shows us what we tend to forget: the world is full of wonder. This vignette also evokes an image of a child emotionally and imaginatively engaged in her world. This is the aim of IEE for students of all ages.

I began this book with the premise that we are not going to be able to address ecological problems without an understanding of the relational nature of the world and, importantly, how we are implicated in the world. As educators, we need to seriously consider how to make teaching and learning more emotionally and imaginatively engaging and how to connect students, through their learning, to the local natural and cultural contexts of which they are part. It is my hope that this book has offered you the tools you need to make this kind of engagement possible for your students. I have also aimed to connect with you as a reader, by employing some of the cognitive tools of IEE (e.g., mental imagery, metaphor, and narrative structure) in the writing. I hope that this leaves you emotionally engaged with the possibilities that IEE offers for developing your students' ecological understanding.

This final chapter offers some specific strategies and tips for developing and sustaining an Imaginative Ecological Education program. The first section discusses assessment and evaluation, the second section lists some tips for starting an IEE approach, and the final section has templates for planning two types of units: mythic and romantic.

Thoughts on Assessment and Evaluation of Student Learning

You might be wondering how assessment and evaluation of student learning can be incorporated into IEE. How can you determine what students have learned? How can you maintain imaginative engagement through the evaluation process? How can you assess how well you are doing at engaging students in learning and cultivating their ecological understanding? While these are not easy questions to answer, it is important to ask them and other questions about evaluation not only to maximize your students' success, but to give you the opportunity to reflect on your teaching practices.

Opportunities for Students to Demonstrate Their Learning

In IEE it is important to consider ways to provide students with opportunities to imaginatively and ecologically demonstrate their learning. By way of example, let's consider some possible ways to conclude the unit on weather discussed in chapters 3 and 4.

We want to finish the weather unit in a way that celebrates the life-giving nature of weather that students have experienced through their learning. Of course, nature may also be viewed as "death-dealing"—though that's perhaps not a great way to put it.

At the end of chapter 4, specific "Honouring" activities are suggested for students to demonstrate what they have learned, build upon their somatic experiences, and celebrate their awareness of their involvement in the world around them. You might also want to give your students opportunities to evoke their awe—and perhaps—their fear of the life-and-death dualism that is at the heart of weather study, in a final project with two dimensions: individual and collaborative. If the unit has been completed over the course of the school year, then there will be a lot of data and experiences for students to include in a final expression of their learning.

Final individual project

Possibilities for final individual projects can draw together students' deepening knowledge of their special places with their knowledge of different aspects of weather. Students can:

- create portfolios that capture in visual and written formats highlights in the year-in-the-life of a "budding" meteorologist—a kind of "Learning in Depth" project for each student;
- use digital images of place taken throughout the course of the year with personal narratives of their learning to create visual exhibitions of the "weather" and how they "weathered the weather"; and/or
- individually participate in a kind of "knowledge fair" in which they, along with their parents, siblings, and teachers, go to their special spots; it is here, in these emotionally charged places, that they can provide insight into what they have learned and experienced. They can "report" on their place—*what's the story?* Unlike a fair in which the knowledge that the student has gained is displayed in a central location, this fair would connect directly with the places in which students have been engaged.

Whatever format a final project takes, returning to the imaginative context in which students have been studying would be wise. Since, in this example, the imaginative context is the life-giving nature of weather, in shaping a final project you might consider appropriate ways students can give thanks for what weather provides. In what thankful ways—ways that show gratitude—can students honour the weather? Teachers can also think of ways students might reveal the currents of danger that run below the surface of the story they've been a part of throughout the unit—how can we all weather the wild world around us? What dangers have students personally experienced (cuts, scrapes, bruises, sprains, scars, scares, etc.) from their outdoor study?

Final collaborative project

A collaborative component of the study can involve students in some collective representation of place and weather. Here are a few ideas:

- a multimodal experience that includes song and dance, poetry and games, and perhaps an audio-visual compilation of all that has been produced in the portfolios and also in the songs, dances, and so on
- a dramatic performance that engages them in role (e.g., as various weather phenomena), a dramatic theatre of the sky, or some other such context for evoking the power and mystery of weather
- a symphony of the sky, representing through sound (and, if necessary, explaining orally or in text) the impact of the various weather phenomena they have been learning about
- a comic demonstration of some of the memorable moments of their training in meteorology

You might bring all these ideas together in a class "variety show" in which students are free to demonstrate their understanding in whatever ways they choose.

It is not my intention to articulate in detail any particular assessment practice. You and your students will collaboratively shape something that suits your teaching and contexts and, importantly, your students' needs and interests. I want only to suggest that the cognitive tools that have shaped the unit be considered in designing assessment and that whatever your students choose to do as a final demonstration of their learning be a celebration of the place, of students' deepening sense of place, and of the sense of community that has developed over the course of the year.

IEE Assessment and Evaluation

What about traditional tests? Because IEE supports the teaching and learning of the regular curriculum, you can assess knowledge in standard ways; for example, by using traditional content tests to determine what students have learned and remembered. But because IEE is concerned with both content *and* students' understanding and imaginative and emotional engagement, appropriate assessment also requires looking for markers of that engagement in students' work. It is my hope that one aspect of the larger impact of imaginative ecological pedagogy will be an expansion of the way teachers conceptualize and practise assessment and evaluation of student learning. If you embrace pedagogical practices that acknowledge the imaginative and emotional lives of children—and the richness of the natural and cultural contexts in which they live and learn—you will want to reconsider the often limiting and limited standardized and placeless nature of most approaches to educational evaluation and assessment.

In the context of IEE, educators encounter a tension between the ways we talk about and enact assessment (particularly in terms of measuring and quantifying student learning) and the features of learning that are *not* quantifiable. How, for example, does one "measure" emotional engagement with place, imaginativeness, or sense of wonder? My first thought is that IEE should be free from current notions of assessment and evaluation. IEE teachers don't need or necessarily want to determine how *imaginative* students are to any standard deviation, mean, median, or mode. Rather, the concern is with students' learning experiences—are they positive? are they wonderful?—*and* with how well teachers are engaging students in learning. In what ways can teachers gain some insight into student engagement and how well they are doing as educators in transforming students' relationships with the natural world? How well has an IEE approach to teaching facilitated the development of students' ecological understanding?

Asking these types of questions leads into difficult terrain, a land where it no longer makes sense—or is even possible—to seek measurements for purposes of comparing and ranking students or schools. The focus becomes what counts as *evidence* of imaginative engagement, emotional connection, sense of place, and ecological understanding. IEE teachers need to consider what methodological approaches are useful for gaining this evidence.

IEE Assessment Practice Guidelines

The following are some guidelines for designing and implementing IEE assessment practice. You may not find any one guideline, on its own, to be particularly groundbreaking. However, taken together, and used to create a context in which to make sense of and describe student learning, these guidelines can offer a radically different and generative way of talking about how well our students and our schools are doing.

1. IEE requires participatory and collaborative forms of student assessment that engage students actively in the process of their own assessment of learning. Therefore, IEE teachers should look for ways to use self-assessment, collaboration, and partnerships, as opposed to competition in the classroom.

2. Teachers should consider the process of learning in addition to student products (e.g., assignments, projects). Students should be given opportunities to reflect on *how* they came to understand topics and, perhaps, what they didn't expect to learn.

3. Teachers should consider unintended student outcomes along with those predetermined by the curriculum.

4. Students should be given opportunities to demonstrate their knowledge in ways that allow for diverse expression of understanding.

5. Teachers should look for indicators that students are more personally engaged with the world: Are they acting differently? Are they talking differently? Are they more concerned with what happens in the world around them? Teachers can also look for indicators that their students have been imaginatively engaged in their lessons: Outside of school/class time, are students talking about what they are learning? Have their parents noticed any changes in students' attitudes? Are students seeking out more information on their own time?

6. Looking at IEE as an overall program, teachers should consider test scores as just one piece of a much larger web of indicators of student learning: Are students flourishing? Are they joyful? Are they taking initiatives in their learning that extend topics into dimensions other than those introduced by the teacher?

Tips for Starting an IEE Approach

If you are inspired to use an IEE approach in your teaching, the following section provides some personal, pedagogical, and administrative suggestions for getting started.

Some Personal Suggestions: What You Need to Know and Do

Become familiar with IEE principles and practices
Spend some time on the IEE website (http://ierg.ca/IEE/) and use the available resources. Become familiar with how IEE is connected to the cultivation of ecological understanding and how any topic can be shaped imaginatively and ecologically.

Think about place

In what place is your school situated? In the context of IEE, this is a crucial question. If your intention is to interest your students in the local natural and cultural contexts in which they live and to engage their imaginations in developing a *sense of place*, it is crucial that you have or actively pursue developing a sense of where you (the school, the students) are in the world. The question, "Where are you?" requires you to know something of the natural world of which you are part: what flora and fauna are native to your area? Where does the water come from? What watershed is the place a part of? You should also know about the cultural context of the place. What's the history of the area? Why are streets or parks named as they are? What traditions are found in this place?

You also need to spend some time developing your own meaning for and emotional connections to place. As you explore the possibilities for connecting your students to the natural world—whether it be in a playground, a local park, or perhaps in a larger natural area (especially in more rural schools)—you can investigate your own feelings about place.

Prepare to move out of your comfort zone

Becoming an imaginative ecological educator will likely draw you into unfamiliar pedagogical terrain. Why? Because this approach requires you to shift away from the pedagogical practices you were trained in. For example, you will consider how to get students outside on a regular basis, how to situate learning in place, and what the place itself can teach you and your students. Prepare to be a different kind of teacher. Prepare to think more about how to emotionally engage your students and how your teaching can help them understand their connectedness within a living world.

Some Pedagogical Suggestions

Engage the emotions and imagination

What's the story here? This question will be one you return to again and again as an imaginative ecological educator. Your pedagogical practice begins with your search for the emotional significance of whatever it is you are teaching. Once you find it, your teaching becomes storytelling. You can teach in a way that connects to this emotional core, leaving your students *feeling* something for what they are learning. You will draw on a variety of tools to engage your students' imaginations in everything they are learning.

Engage the body

How does the body "understand" the topic? In what ways can the body's learning tools—including the senses, the emotions, the sense of musicality and pattern, humour, and gesture—be engaged in learning? As you educate for ecological understanding, you will look for ways to support your students' comprehension of how their bodies engage in the world around them as they learn all aspects of the curriculum.

Engage with place

As an imaginative ecological educator, you will consider what the topics you are teaching mean in a specific place and what that place can contribute to students' understanding of any topic. You will aim to engage students' imaginative interests in forming emotional attachments to aspects of their immediate environments (primary and elementary) or exploring and creating special places (middle and secondary).

Some Administrative Suggestions: Establishing Networks of Support

Seek administrative support

Consider gaining the support of your school administration for introducing IEE. With the backing of administration, you will have an easier time taking students outdoors for learning. You might want to explain the theoretical and practical dimensions of your IEE practice so that administrators understand the pedagogical value of what you are doing. (You can explain that, through an IEE approach, students will both fulfill regular curricular requirements and do so in emotionally and imaginatively engaging ways.) Many schools now include in their mission statements a desire to increase students' ecological understanding. Unfortunately, there is a shortage of suitable resources and pedagogy to effectively do so. Your administration might be pleased to learn that there is support for teachers in dealing with ecological issues, particularly for teachers implementing an IEE approach.

Seek parental support

Talk to your students' parents about your intention to make their children's learning both imaginative and ecological. They will want to know that their child's individual learning needs will be met. You can assure them that IEE represents a way to do so. (Indeed, students learn and remember more when they are meaningfully engaged. By framing teaching around emotional engagement, teachers can support all students' learning.) Let parents know that their children will be going outside frequently. You might ask them to provide suitable clothing and footwear for cold or wet weather—rubber boots and a change of clothes might be kept at school for each child. Parents can also provide you with information about any potential allergies their child may have to plants, insects, bee stings, and so on. Be sure to keep a record of such allergies and have the necessary antidotes on hand at all times.

Collect resources

Before you start an IEE program, identify the physical tools and resources that can support your students' outdoor studies. These items might include

- gardening gloves (you can use clothes pegs to keep the gloves together in pairs);
- plastic bags (for kneeling, sitting, or collecting);

- small containers, plastic tubs, and/or buckets (empty margarine containers with lids work well);
- shovels;
- magnifying glasses;
- rain ponchos (these can be bought inexpensively);
- small notebooks for observations (you can use recycled paper to make your own booklets or buy notebooks with both unlined pages for sketching and lined pages for writing);
- coloured pencils;
- clipboards;
- digital cameras (a few that can be shared); and
- personal flotation devices (PFDs) (a few that can be shared by students who are walking in or near creeks).

Some of these items may already be part of students' school supply lists. Others, such as digital cameras and PFDs, might be donated or bought at a discount from suppliers who support ecological education.

Templates for Teaching

Figures 1 and 2 provide two teaching templates that can be used to plan units that fulfill the triad of IEE principles. Figure 1 primarily uses mythic cognitive tools and will be most useful for teachers of early or non-readers. Figure 2 employs romantic cognitive tools and will be of interest to anyone teaching children in late elementary through middle school. Outlines of these templates are provided in Appendix A so that you can adapt them as needed.

FIGURE 1. IMAGINATIVE ECOLOGICAL EDUCATION—MYTHIC PLANNING

1. **Locating importance**

   What is emotionally engaging about this topic? How can it evoke wonder? Why should it matter to you and your students?

2. **Shaping the lesson or unit**

   Teaching shares some features with news reporting. Just as a reporter's aim is to select and shape events to clearly bring out their meaning and emotional importance for readers or listeners, your aim as a teacher is to present your topic in a way that engages the emotions and imaginations of students. To do so, consider which of the following dimensions of students' emotional and imaginative lives can be used to shape your lesson or unit. All of these approaches are related to the skills a good reporter works with.

   2.1. **Finding the story**

   What's the story on the topic? How can you shape the content to reveal its emotional significance?

2.2. Finding binary opposites

What binary opposites best capture the wonder and emotion of the topic? What are the opposing forces in your "story"? What parts of the topic most dramatically embody the binary opposites?

2.3. Finding images

What images best capture the dramatic contrast of the binary opposites?

2.4. Employing additional cognitive tools of mythic understanding

What kinds of activities might employ other tools in your students' cognitive toolkits? Consider the following:

- Puzzles and mystery: How could students explore some aspects of the mystery attached to the topic? What puzzles might they wonder about?
- Metaphors: How might students employ metaphors in deepening their understanding of the topic?
- Jokes and humour: Could students create their own jokes about the topic? How might they expand their understanding through what is humorous about the topic?
- Rhyme, rhythm, and pattern: Are there patterns in the topic students could play with? What activities might draw attention to rhyme, rhythm, and pattern?
- Games, drama, and play: How can students engage in games, drama, and play in learning about the topic?
- Embryonic tools of romantic understanding: In what ways can students engage with the heroic and human dimensions of the topic? What kinds of activities might reveal its extremes? How can these aspects draw students forward in their thinking about the topic?

3. Engaging the body: Activeness

How does the body participate in this story? What activities can engage the learner somatically in learning the content of the story? How can students' sense of relation be engaged? What other cognitive tools support the child's sense of embeddedness in the world?

4. Engaging with context: Sense of place

How can students learn about the topic in a way that engages them emotionally and imaginatively with some aspect of the natural world around them? How does the topic connect to the local environment? What does the topic mean in this place?

5. Resources

What resources can you use to learn more about the topic and to shape your story? What resources are useful in creating activities? What resources can you suggest to students?

6. Conclusion

How does the story end? How can the conflict set up between the binary opposites be resolved in a satisfying way? Alternatively, what new questions emerge as students make sense of these opposing forces? What aspect of the topic might draw students forward in wonder?

7. Evaluation

How can you know whether the topic has been understood, its importance grasped, and the content learned?

FIGURE 2. IMAGINATIVE ECOLOGICAL EDUCATION—ROMANTIC PLANNING

1. Identifying "heroic" qualities

What heroic human qualities are central to the topic? What emotional images do they evoke? What aspect of the topic can best evoke wonder?

2. Shaping the lesson or unit

Teaching shares some features with news reporting. Just as a reporter's aim is to select and shape events to clearly bring out their meaning and emotional importance for readers or listeners, your aim as a teacher is to present your topic in a way that engages the emotions and imaginations of students. To do so, consider which of the following dimensions of students' emotional and imaginative lives can be used to shape your lesson or unit. All of these approaches are related to the skills a good reporter works with.

2.1. Finding the story or narrative

What's the story on the topic? How can the narrative illustrate the heroic qualities of the topic?

2.2. Finding extremes and limits

What aspects of the topic expose extremes of experience or limits of reality? What is most exotic, bizarre, or strange about the topic?

2.3. Finding connections to human hopes, fears, and passions

To what human hopes, fears, and passions does the topic connect? What ideals and/or challenges to conventions are evident in the content? Through what human emotions can students access the topic?

2.4. Employing additional cognitive tools of romantic understanding

What kinds of activities might you design to employ other tools in students' cognitive toolkits? Consider the following:

- Collections and hobbies: What parts of the topic can students explore in exhaustive detail? What activity might engage students in learning everything they can about some aspect of the topic?
- Change of context: What kinds of activities could change the context in the classroom? How might drama or role play be employed or how might students engage the body's senses in learning?
- The literate eye: How could graphs, lists, flowcharts, or other visual formats be used in learning about the topic?
- The sense of wonder: What kind of activity might evoke students' sense of wonder? How could you use that sense of wonder to draw students forward in thinking about further dimensions of the topic?
- Embryonic tools of philosophic understanding: How might you frame the topic in terms of a general idea or theory? How can students begin to move from the particular aspects of what they have been learning to a more general explanation? How can students' sense of agency be engaged?

2.5. Drawing on tools of mythic understanding

How might students use some of the tools of mythic understanding in learning about the topic? How might abstract and affective binary opposites, metaphor, vivid mental imagery, humour, puzzles, and sense of mystery be employed?

3. Engaging the body: Activeness

How does the body participate in this story? What activities can engage the learner somatically in learning the content of the story? How can students' sense of relation be engaged? What other cognitive tools support the child's sense of embeddedness in the world?

4. Engaging with context: Sense of place

What aspect of the topic might be learned in a way that affords students the opportunity to explore the natural world around them? How might learning about the topic support a sense of belonging in the natural environment?

5. Resources

What resources can you use to learn more about the topic and to shape your story? What resources are useful in creating activities? What resources can you suggest to students?

6. Conclusion

How does the narrative end? How can you best bring the topic to a satisfactory closure and how can students feel satisfaction? Alternatively, what new questions can draw students to think more deeply about the topic? How can you extend students' sense of wonder?

7. Evaluation

How can you know that the content has been learned and understood, and has engaged and stimulated students' imaginations?

These templates should be viewed as flexible guidelines, not rigid frameworks.[1] You might think of these suggestions as threads that you can weave into your teaching to create imaginative contexts for your lessons. Do the threads need to be woven in any particular order? Yes and no. Yes, because it is important to begin by determining what *your* emotional connection is with the topic. That is, the things that evoke *your* sense of wonder will be the basis for the imaginative context you will create for your students. If you identify this source of emotional significance at the outset, you will have the context for using all of the other tools. However, the cognitive tools listed in the templates need not be employed in a specific order.

Additional resources for your IEE teaching are included at the end of the book: Appendix B provides a five-step guide for collaboratively planning imaginative and ecological units and Appendix C provides four templates for IEE unit and lesson planning.

Where to Go from Here?

Consider this an invitation to get involved with the IEE team at Simon Fraser University in British Columbia (http://ierg.ca/IEE/). We are a diverse group of educators who are investigating the theoretical and practical dimensions of imaginative and ecological education. We would welcome the opportunity to hear from you. If you have unanswered questions, please contact me at gcj@sfu.ca or engage in more widespread discussion by adding your question to our discussion thread at http://ierg.ca. Do you have examples of imaginative and ecological teaching (ideas, activities, and so on) that you would like to share? Do you want more ideas? Do you want to collaborate on designing ecological and imaginative features of a new approach to assessment and evaluation?

What I have aimed to show throughout this book is that IEE can offer teachers something that is unique. IEE is unique in its central aim: the cultivation of an emotional and imaginative engagement with place. IEE is unique in its applicability across school contexts and grade levels. It is suitable for teachers in *all* schools: teachers who work in mainstream schools (K–12) who either have a personal interest in cultivating ecological understanding or are part of a staff-wide initiative to do so; teachers who work in schools specifically aimed at cultivating ecological understanding; and teachers who currently use nature as the classroom most, if not all, of the time. IEE is an interdisciplinary approach that focuses centrally on engaging students' imaginations in learning; *all* learning is improved as a result. Because it departs from more traditional, objectives-based approaches to teaching, which continue to dominate in both mainstream classrooms and ecologically oriented ones, IEE also contributes to a much-needed discussion about how educators conceive of human intellectual development and how we can teach in ways that acknowledge the emotional and imaginative lives of students. As discussed in chapter 1, even learning contexts that describe themselves as ecological often continue to be informed by objectives-based approaches that fail to acknowledge the central roles of emotional and imaginative engagement in learning. The Imaginative Ecological Education approach offers a unique alternative.

APPENDIX A

SOME GUIDELINES FOR MYTHIC AND ROMANTIC IEE PLANNING

Imaginative Ecological Education—Mythic Planning

1. Locating importance

2. Shaping the lesson or unit
    2.1. Finding the story

    2.2. Finding binary opposites

    2.3. Finding images

2.4. Employing additional cognitive tools of mythic understanding:

- Puzzles and mystery

- Metaphors

- Jokes and humour

- Rhyme, rhythm, and pattern

- Games, drama, and play

- Embryonic tools of romantic understanding

3. Engaging the body: Activeness

4. Engaging with context: Sense of place

5. Resources

6. Conclusion

7. Evaluation

Imaginative Ecological Education—Romantic Planning

1. Identifying "heroic" qualities

2. Shaping the lesson or unit

    2.1. Finding the story or narrative

    2.2. Finding extremes and limits

    2.3. Finding connections to human hopes, fears, and passions

    2.4. Employing additional cognitive tools of romantic understanding

      - Collections and hobbies

      - Change of context

      - The literate eye

      - The sense of wonder

      - Embryonic tools of philosophic understanding

    2.5. Drawing on tools of mythic understanding

3. **Engaging the body: Activeness**

4. **Engaging with context: Sense of place**

5. **Resources**

6. **Conclusion**

7. **Evaluation**

APPENDIX B

FIVE STEPS FOR COLLABORATIVELY PLANNING IEE UNITS

The following are guidelines for collaboratively planning a unit that can engage students' bodies, emotions, and imaginations in place.

Feeling

Step One. Begin individually. Before you meet as a group to discuss your planning, think carefully about the topic. Step back from it. Ask yourself: What's this topic about? What is it *really* about? What thread runs through it? If you don't know, read and dig deeper. What is your sense of what is significant about it? Hint: What interests you? What engages you? What evokes *your* sense of wonder? Dwell on the topic with your emotions alert. What engages *you*?

> **TIPS:**
> ★ If you are shaping your unit for younger (exclusively oral language using) students, when you identify the emotional quality that runs through the topic consider also the dramatic tension within the topic. What set of binary opposites could be used to shape the unit of study?
> ★ If you are shaping your unit for older (developing or strongly literate) students, try to seek the emotional human quality that runs through the topic, looking, for example, at heroic qualities related to the topic.

Step Two. Collaborate. Share your thoughts and feelings about the topic. During this phase in the planning process team members can describe the "story"—that is, the story form or *emotional idea* that they think could maintain the unit of study and the content that needs to be taught. Get feedback from each other. Which ideas seem to be most engaging and most suitable to sustain the unit?

Step Three. Once you have determined your story for the unit or topic, look at the content you wish to teach through the different cognitive tools. How might you convey content in a way that engages these tools? Refer to figures 1 and 2 in chapter 8 (pages 117–119) and work through the planning charts in Appendix A. Discuss ways that different cognitive tools might be employed to continue to clarify and illuminate your story. Ask yourself: How can using this cognitive tool deepen students' understanding of the story and the emotional meaning of the topic?

Activeness

Step Four. As a group, brainstorm how the body participates—or could participate—in understanding different aspects of the topic. How can you engage the senses and dwell on the emotional responses these evoke? How can you draw students' attention to the human body's particular way of knowing this topic? Could the body be used—through form or gesture—to convey different emotionally charged meanings?

Sense of Place

Step Five. If possible, take your planning outside. Be thoughtful about the possibilities for teaching and learning that your local place offers you and your students. What does the topic mean in this place? In what ways can students deepen their understanding of this place through learning about the topic? How can students be afforded opportunities to develop emotional associations with particular locations? How can students be afforded opportunities to explore—literally or metaphorically—the unique features of this place?

Appendix C

TEMPLATES FOR IEE PLANNING

IEE Planning—Overview of Teaching for Feeling

Use the following charts to plan how you will include cognitive tools in your teaching units. Try to include, for each unit, as many cognitive tools as you can; the more you do, the more engaged your students will be. You can make brief notes here of how you plan to employ different cognitive tools and then use the more detailed lesson-by-lesson format to elaborate.

TOOLS OF ORAL LANGUAGE—MYTHIC UNDERSTANDING	UNIT NAME/TOPIC:	UNIT NAME/TOPIC:	UNIT NAME/TOPIC:
The story form			
Binary opposites			
Jokes and humour			
Mental imagery evoked from words			
Rhyme, rhythm, and pattern			
Sense of mystery and puzzles			
Games, drama, and play			

TOOLS OF WRITTEN LANGUAGE—ROMANTIC UNDERSTANDING	UNIT NAME/TOPIC:	UNIT NAME/TOPIC:	UNIT NAME/TOPIC:
Narrative structuring			
Heroic qualities			
Sense of wonder			
Humanizing meaning			
Extremes of experience and limits of reality			
Collecting and organizing			
The literate eye			
Change of context and role play			

IEE Planning—Teaching Overview

Use this table to think about and plan how you will engage the IEE principles across your teaching units and/or subject areas.

UNIT OR SUBJECT AREA	FEELING PRINCIPLE	ACTIVENESS PRINCIPLE	SENSE OF PLACE PRINCIPLE
(e.g., Creative Writing or Mathematics)	Have you considered the emotional significance of the topic? What is the story? Do activities employ students' cognitive tools and leave them emotionally engaged?	How can you engage students' bodies in learning about unit topics? How can learning activities draw students' attention to their physical involvement in the world?	Are learning activities connected to the local natural and cultural contexts? How can the place contribute to students' understanding of topics?

IEE Planning—Unit Overview (Lessons at a Glance)

Use this table to plan how you will include cognitive tools in your teaching units. You need not fulfill each principle in each lesson but you should aim to address them all during the unit and, if possible, at least one principle per lesson.

UNIT OR SUBJECT AREA	FEELING PRINCIPLE	ACTIVENESS PRINCIPLE	SENSE OF PLACE PRINCIPLE
	Have you considered the emotional significance of the topic? What is the story? Do activities employ students' cognitive tools and leave them emotionally engaged?	How can you engage students' bodies in learning about unit topics? How can learning activities draw students' attention to their physical involvement in the world?	Are learning activities connected to the local natural and cultural contexts? How can the place contribute to students' understanding of topics?
Lesson 1:			
Lesson 2:			
Lesson 3:			
Lesson 4:			
Lesson 5:			

Notes

Introduction

1. Blenkinsop, "Imaginative Ecological Education"; Traina and Darley-Hill, *Perspectives in Bioregional Education.*
2. Hacking and Barratt, "Editorial"; Nabhan and Trimble, *Geography of Childhood*; Palmer, "Development of Concern for the Environment"; Palmer and Neal, *Handbook of Environmental Education*; Tanner, "Significant Life Experiences."
3. Orr, "Recollection," 105.
4. Kagawa and Selby, *Education and Climate Change.*
5. For a more detailed theoretical account of IEE, see Judson, *New Approach to Ecological Education.*
6. The examples presented in this book were developed with the support of funding from the Social Sciences and Humanities Resource Council of Canada, grant 833-2009-4005, "Aligning Education and Sustainability in Maple Ridge, BC: A Study of Place-Based Ecological Schooling."

Chapter 1

1. Support for these initiatives include, for example, Grant and Littlejohn's series of *Teaching Green* manuals designed for primary and secondary teachers. These resource manuals outline different activities that teachers can use to engage students with the natural world while they fulfill prescribed learning outcomes in different curricular areas.
2. For information on the Coombes School in West Berkshire, UK, and its history, see Rowe and Humphries, *Coombes Approach.*
3. See, for example, "Mother Earth Kindergarten" (Webber, "School without Walls").

4. Webber, "School without Walls."

5. For more information on the Maple Ridge Environmental School project, see http://es.sd42.ca.

6. Knight, *Forest Schools for All*, 2.

7. See note 6 above.

8. Constable, *Outdoor Classroom*; Slade, Lowery, and Bland, "Evaluating the Impact of Forest Schools."

9. Hill, "Developing Approaches to Outdoor Education," 15.

10. See note 9 above.

11. Ridgers, Knowles, and Sayers, "Encouraging Play in the Natural Environment."

12. Slade, Lowery, and Bland, "Evaluating the Impact of Forest Schools," 66.

13. Louv, *Last Child in the Woods*; ibid., *The Nature Principle*.

14. See note 13 above.

15. Berry, *Evening Thoughts*; Blenkinsop, "Imaginative Ecological Education"; Bookchin, *Ecology of Freedom*; Hutchison, *Growing Up Green*; Orr, *Down to the Wire*; Orr, *Hope Is an Imperative*; Selby, "Darker Shade of Green"; Selby, "Signature of the Whole"; and Snyder, *Gary Snyder Reader*.

16. See note 13 above.

17. Traina, "Challenge of Bioregional Education."

18. Egan, *Educated Mind*.

19. See Callahan, *Education and the Cult of Efficiency*, for a discussion of the application of industrial systems to teaching.

20. Eisner, *Educational Imagination*.

21. See note 20 above.

22. Tyler, *Basic Principles of Curriculum*.

23. See note 18 above.

24. Hill, Wilson, and Watson, "Learning Ecology"; O'Sullivan and Taylor, *Learning toward an Ecological Consciousness*; and Sewall, "Skill of Ecological Perception."

25. Egan, *Imagination in Teaching and Learning*; Greene, "What Happened to Imagination?"

26. Buber, *I and Thou*.

27. Fox, *Toward a Transpersonal Ecology*; Naess, *Life's Philosophy*; and Naess and Rothenberg, *Ecology, Community and Lifestyle*.

28. Bertling, "Exercising the Ecological Imagination."

29. Takahashi, "Personal and Social Transformation."

30. Bertling, "Exercising the Ecological Imagination"; Blenkinsop, "Seeds of Green"; Judson, *New Approach to Ecological Education*; Judson, *Imagination in Mind*; Judson, "Re-Imagining Sustainability Education"; and Takahashi, "Personal and Social Transformation."

31. See note 28 above.

Chapter 2

1. Judson, *New Approach to Ecological Education*; O'Sullivan and Taylor, *Learning toward an Ecological Consciousness*; and Stone and Barlow, *Ecological Literacy*.

2. Smith and Williams, *Ecological Education in Action*, 3.

3. See note 2 above.

4. Egan, *Educated Mind*; ibid., *Imaginative Approach to Teaching*.

5. Bingham and Sidorkin, *No Education without Relation*; Noddings, *Challenge to Care in Schools*; and Sidorkin, *Learning Relations*.

6. Eisner, *Educational Imagination*.

7. Ong, *Orality and Literacy*.

8. Naess, *Life's Philosophy*.

9. Ardoin, "Interdisciplinary Understanding of Place."

10. Tuan, *Man and Nature*; ibid., *Space and Place*.

11. Seamon and Mugerauer, *Dwelling, Place, and Environment*.

12. Smith, "Place-Based Education: Learning"; ibid., "Place-Based Education: Breaking Through."

13. Piersol, "Our Hearts Leap Up."

14. Smith, "Place-Based Education: Learning"; ibid., "Place-Based Education: Breaking Through"; ibid., "Place-Based Education"; and Smith and Sobel, *Place- and Community-Based Education*.

15. Judson, *New Approach to Ecological Education*; ibid., *Imagination in Mind*; Fettes and Judson, "Imagination and the Cognitive Tools."

16. Judson, *New Approach to Ecological Education*.

17. The Environmental School Project—located in Maple Ridge, BC, Canada—offers students place-based, imaginative, and ecological approaches to education. While officially opened to students in 2011, our research team began work on the project in 2008. The project is funded through an environmental Community-University Research Alliance grant (eCURA) from the Social Sciences and Humanities Research Council of Canada (SSHRC). To learn more, visit http://es.sd42.ca.

Chapter 3

1. Egan, *Educated Mind*.

2. Ibid.

3. Ibid.

4. First published in *Tatler* magazine in 1710.

5. From *A Complete Collection of Polite and Ingenious Conversation*, published in 1738.

6. Abram, *Spell of the Sensuous*, 230.

7. Ibid., 233. Note that Abram cites extensively from James Kale McNeley's book: *Holy Wind in Navajo Philosophy*.

8. Glickman, *Glossary of Meteorology*.

9. *Wikipedia*, s.v. "Storm Chasers," http://en.wikipedia.org/wiki/Storm_chasing (last modified July 6, 2014).

10. Abram, *Spell of the Sensuous*, 225.

11. Ibid., 226.

12. Ibid., 228.

13. Ibid., 228.

Chapter 4

1. For a detailed and more theoretical discussion of the activeness principle and the contributions of somatic understanding for ecological understanding, see Judson, *New Approach to Ecological Education*.
2. Egan, *Educated Mind*.
3. Mithen, *Singing Neanderthals*.
4. Radha, *Hatha Yoga*, 28.
5. Ibid., 252.
6. Ibid., 118.
7. Ibid., 146.
8. Ibid., 102.
9. Ibid., 105.
10. Abram, *Spell of the Sensuous*, 26.
11. Ibid., 99.
12. Ibid., 99.
13. Atsma, "Boreas."
14. Mount Washington Observatory, "Story of World Record Wind."
15. National Oceanic and Atmospheric Administration, "Extremely Powerful Hurricane Katrina."
16. Ibid.

Chapter 5

1. Smith, "Place-Based Education: Learning"; Ibid., Place-Based Education: Breaking Through"; Smith and Sobel, "Place- and Community-Based Education."
2. Judson, *New Approach to Ecological Education*; Ibid., *Imagination in Mind*; Ibid., *Re-Imagining Sustainability Education*.
3. For a detailed description of place-making cognitive tools, please refer to Judson, *New Approach to Ecological Education*, 73–95.
4. For more information on place-making cognitive tools see: Judson, *New Approach to Ecological Education*; Ibid., *Imagination in Mind*; Fettes and Judson, "Imagination and the Cognitive Tools of Place-Making."
5. Strich, "Reflective Sit Spots."
6. Ibid., 23–24.
7. Judson, "Imaginative Ecological Education."
8. Egan, *Learning in Depth*.
9. Egan, *Whole School Projects*.

Chapter 6

1. Bennett, "Indian 'Shadow Wolves' "; *Wikipedia*, s.v. "Shadow Wolves," http://en.wikipedia.org/wiki/Shadow_Wolves (last modified April 26, 2014).
2. Abram, *Spell of the Sensuous*, 129.
3. For further detail see Van Matre, *Acclimatizing*.

4. Brown, in "Meditations on an Apple," combines the story of the apple with sensory engagement. It is an example of how "the story of a single apple [can become] a whole curriculum in ecological literacy" (p. 184). While Brown's work focuses on the history of the apple, it also demonstrates how it is possible to invoke wonder and awe by taking the time to examine something closely.

5. For more details on ecological monitoring activities and how these can be systematically included in teaching, see: Kaucheck and Marcinkowski, "Biological Monitoring Programs."

6. See Ellis, "Tales from the Trail."

Chapter 7

Special thanks to Laura Piersol for her participation in writing activities in this chapter and for her ongoing encouragement. It was a joy collaborating with her in Maple Ridge, BC. She developed the following activities: "The Deer's View; The Photographer's View"; "Awaken the Senses!"; "Stalking"; and "Rock On! Of Rocks and Living Things."

1. Abram, *Spell of the Sensuous*, 133.

2. Ibid.

3. From "Auguries of Innocence," stanza 1, in *The Ballads (or Pickering) Manuscript*, c. 1801–03.

4. Schafer, *Soundscape*.

Chapter 8

1. Circular forms of these templates, which many teachers find useful for initial planning, are available on the IEE website under "Teacher Resources": http://ierg.ca/IEE/

REFERENCES

Abram, David. *The Spell of the Sensuous*. New York: Vintage Books, 1996.

Ammons, Doug. *Whitewater Philosophy*. Missoula, MT: Water Nymph Press, 2009.

Ardoin, Nicole M. "Toward an Interdisciplinary Understanding of Place: Lessons for Environmental Education." *Canadian Journal of Environmental Education* 11 (2006): 112–126.

Atsma, Aaron. "Boreas." *Theoi Greek Mythology*. Accessed June 19, 2014. http://www.theoi.com/Titan/AnemosBoreas.html.

Bennett, Brian. "Indian 'Shadow Wolves' Stalk Smugglers on Arizona Reservation." *Los Angeles Times*, November 21, 2011. Accessed February 6, 2015. http://articles.latimes.com/2011/nov/21/nation/la-na-adv-shadow-wolves-20111122.

Berry, Thomas. *Evening Thoughts: Reflecting on Earth as Sacred Community*. San Francisco: Sierra Club Books, 2006.

Bertling, Joy. "Exercising the Ecological Imagination: Representing the Future of Place. *Art Education* 66 (2013): 33–39.

Bingham, Charles W., and Alexander M. Sidorkin. *No Education Without Relation*. New York: Peter Lang, 2004.

Blenkinsop, Sean. "Seeds of Green: My Own Arctic Copper/Mine." *Canadian Journal of Environmental Education* 11, no. 1 (2006): 157–165.

———. "Imaginative Ecological Education: Six Necessary Components." In *Imagination 360°: Effective Learning through the Imagination*, edited by Gillian Judson, 139–148. Rotterdam: Sense Publishers, 2008.

Bookchin, Murray. *The Ecology of Freedom: The Emergence and Dissolution of Hierarchy*. Montreal: Black Rose Books, 1991.

Brown, Janet. "Meditations on an Apple." In *Ecological Literacy: Educating Our Children for a Sustainable World*, edited by Michael K. Stone and Zenobia Barlow, 184–189. San Francisco: Sierra Club Books, 2005.

Buber, Martin. *I and Thou [Ich und Du]*. 2nd ed., translated by R. G. Smith. New York: Scribner, 1958.

Callahan, Raymond E. *Education and the Cult of Efficiency*. Chicago: University of Chicago Press, 1964.

Constable, Karen. *The Outdoor Classroom Ages 3–7: Using Ideas from Forest Schools to Enrich Learning*. New York: Routledge, 2012.

Dillard, Anne. *Pilgrim at Tinker Creek*. 1st U.S. ed. New York: Harper's Magazine Press, 1974.

Egan, Kieran. *Imagination in Teaching and Learning: The Middle School Years*. Chicago: University of Chicago Press, 1992.

———. *The Educated Mind: How Cognitive Tools Shape Our Understanding*. Chicago: University of Chicago Press, 1997.

———. *An Imaginative Approach to Teaching*. San Francisco: Jossey-Bass, 2005.

———. *Learning in Depth: A Simple Innovation That Can Transform Schooling*. Chicago: University of Chicago Press, 2010.

———. *Whole School Projects: Engaging Imaginations through Interdisciplinary Inquiry*. With Bob Dunton and Gillian Judson. New York: Teachers College Press, 2014.

Eisner, Elliot W. *The Educational Imagination: On the Design and Evaluation of School Programs*. Upper Saddle River, NJ: Prentice Hall, 2002.

Ellis, Brian. "Tales from the Trail." *Green Teacher* 90 (2010): 22–25.

Fettes, Mark, and Gillian Judson. "Imagination and the Cognitive Tools of Place-Making." *Journal of Environmental Education* 42, no. 2 (2011): 123–135.

Fox, Warwick. *Toward a Transpersonal Ecology: Developing New Foundations for Environmentalism*. Boston: Shambhala, 1990.

Glickman, Todd S., ed. *Glossary of Meteorology*. 2nd ed. Boston: American Meteorological Society, 2000.

Grant, Tim, and Gail Littlejohn, eds. *Teaching Green—The Middle Years: Hands-on Learning in Grades 6–8*. Gabriola Island, BC: New Society Publishers, 2004.

———. *Teaching Green—The Elementary Years: Hands-on Learning in Grades K–5*. Gabriola Island, BC: New Society Publishers, 2005.

———. *Teaching Green—The High School Years: Hands-on Learning in Grades 9–12*. Gabriola Island, BC: New Society Publishers, 2009.

Greene, Maxine. "What Happened to Imagination?" In *Imagination and Education*, edited by Kieran Egan and Dan Nadaner, 45–56. New York: Teachers College Press, 1988.

Hacking, Elisabeth C., and Robert Barratt. "Editorial." *Environmental Education Review* 13, no. 4 (2007): 419–23.

Hill, Allen. "Developing Approaches to Outdoor Education That Promote Sustainability Education." *Australian Journal of Outdoor Education* 16 (2012): 19–31.

Hill, Stuart B., Steve Wilson, and Kevin Watson. "Learning Ecology: A New Approach to Learning and Transforming Ecological Consciousness." In *Learning Toward an Ecological Consciousness: Selected Transformative Practices*, edited by Edmund O'Sullivan and Marilyn M. Taylor, 47–64. New York: Palgrave Macmillan, 2004.

Hutchison, David. *Growing Up Green: Education for Ecological Renewal*. New York: Teachers College Press, 1998.

Judson, Gillian. "Imaginative Ecological Education." PhD diss., Simon Fraser University, 2008.

———. *A New Approach to Ecological Education: Engaging Students' Imaginations in Their World*. New York: Peter Lang, 2010.

———. *Imagination in Mind: Educating for Ecological Literacy*. Seminar Series Paper 198 (September). Melbourne: Centre for Strategic Education, 2010.

———. "Re-Imagining Sustainability Education: Emotional and Imaginative Engagement in Learning." In *Sustainability Frontiers: Critical and Transformative Voices from the Borderlands of Sustainability Education*, edited by Fumiyo Kagawa and David Selby. Farmington Hills, MI: Barbara Budrich Publishers, 2014.

Kagawa, Fumiyo, and David Selby. "Introduction." In *Education and Climate Change: Living and Learning in Interesting Times*, edited by Fumiyo Kagawa and David Selby, 1–11. New York: Routledge, 2010.

Kaucheck, Lynna Marie, and Thomas Marcinkowski. "Biological Monitoring Programs for K–12 Students." *Green Teacher* 90 (2010): 26–32.

Knight, Sara, ed. *Forest School for All*. London: Sage Publications, 2011.

Lopez, Barry. *Arctic Dreams: Imagination and Desire in a Northern Landscape*. New York: Scribner, 1986.

Louv, Richard. *Last Child in the Woods: Saving Our Children from Nature-Deficit Disorder*. Chapel Hill, NC: Algonquin Books, 2005.

———. *The Nature Principle: Human Restoration and the End of Nature-Deficit Disorder*. Chapel Hill, NC: Algonquin Books, 2011.

McNeley, James Kale. *Holy Wind in Navajo Philosophy*. Tucson: University of Arizona Press, 1981.

Mithen, Steven. *The Singing Neanderthals: The Origins of Music, Language, Mind and Body*. London: Weidenfeld & Nicolson, 2005.

Mount Washington Observatory. "The Story of the World Record Wind." Accessed June 19, 2014. http://www.mountwashington.org/about/visitor/recordwind.php.

Nabhan, Gary P., and Stephen Trimble. *The Geography of Childhood: Why Children Need Wild Places*. Boston: Beacon Press, 1994.

Naess, Arne. *Life's Philosophy: Reason and Feeling in a Deeper World*. Athens, GA: University of Georgia Press, 2002.

Naess, Arne, and David Rothenberg. *Ecology, Community and Lifestyle: Outline of an Ecosophy*. Cambridge: Cambridge University Press, 1989.

National Oceanic and Atmospheric Administration. "Extremely Powerful Hurricane Katrina Leaves a Historic Mark on the Northern Gulf Coast." Accessed June 19, 2014. http://www.srh.noaa.gov/mob/?n=katrina.

Noddings, Nel. *The Challenge to Care in Schools: An Alternative Approach to Education*. New York: Teachers College Press, 1992.

———. "The Caring Teacher." In *Handbook of Research on Teaching*, edited by Virginia Richardson, 99–105. Washington: American Educational Research Association, 2001.

Ong, Walter J. *Orality and Literacy: The Technologizing of the Word*. London: Methuen, 1982.

Orr, David W. "Recollection." In *Ecological Literacy: Educating Our Children for a Sustainable World*, edited by Michael. K. Stone and Zenobia Barlow, 96–106. San Francisco: Sierra Club Books, 2005.

———. *Down to the Wire: Confronting Climate Collapse*. Oxford: Oxford University Press, 2009.

———. *Hope Is an Imperative: The Essential David Orr*. Washington: Island Press, 2011.

O'Sullivan, Edmund, and Marilyn M. Taylor. *Learning Toward an Ecological Consciousness: Selected Transformative Practices*. New York: Palgrave Macmillan, 2004.

Palmer, Joy A. "Development of Concern for the Environment and Formative Experiences of Educators." *The Journal of Environmental Education* 24 (1993): 26–30.

Palmer, Joy A., and Philip Neal. *The Handbook of Environmental Education*. London: Routledge, 1994.

Piersol, Laura. "Our Hearts Leap Up: Awakening Wonder within the Classroom." In *Wonder-Full Education: The Centrality of Wonder in Teaching and Learning Across the Curriculum*, edited by Kieran Egan, Annabella Cant, and Gillian Judson, 3–21. New York: Routledge, 2014.

Radha, Sivananda. *Hatha Yoga: The Hidden Language*. Spokane, WA: Timeless Books, 1996.

Ridgers, Nicola D., Zoe R. Knowles, and Jo Sayers. "Encouraging Play in the Natural Environment: A Child-focused Case Study of Forest School." *Children's Geographies* 10, no. 1 (2012): 49–65.

Rowe Susan, and Susan Humphries. *The Coombes Approach: Learning through an Experiential and Outdoor Curriculum*. New York: Continuum, 2012.

Schafer, R. Murray. *Soundscape: Our Sonic Environment and the Tuning of the World*. Rochester, VT: Destiny Books, 1994.

Seamon, David, and Robert Mugerauer, eds. *Dwelling, Place, and Environment: Towards a Phenomenology of Person and World*. Malabar: Krieger, 2000.

Selby, David. "A Darker Shade of Green: The Importance of Ecological Thinking in Global Education and School Reform." *Theory into Practice* 39, no. 2, (2000): 88–97.

———. "The Signature of the Whole: Radical Interconnectedness and Its Implications for Global and Environmental Education." In *Expanding the Boundaries of Transformative Learning*, edited by Edmund O'Sullivan, Amish Morrell, and Mary Ann O'Connor, 77–94. New York: Palgrave, 2002.

Sewall, Laura. "The Skill of Ecological Perception." In *Ecopsychology: Restoring the Earth, Healing the Mind*, edited by Theodore Roszak, Mary E. Gomes, and Allen D. Kanner, 201–215. San Francisco: Sierra Club Books, 1995.

Sidorkin, Alexander M. *Learning Relations: Impure Education, Deschooled Schools, and Dialogue with Evil*. New York: Peter Lang, 2002.

Slade, Melanie, Claire Lowery, and Ken Bland. "Evaluating the Impact of Forest Schools: A Collaboration between a University and a Primary School." *Support for Learning: British Journal of Learning Support* 28, no. 2 (2013): 66–72.

Smith, Gregory A. "Place-Based Education: Learning to Be Where We Are." *Phi Delta Kappan* 83 (2002): 584–594.

———. "Place-Based Education: Breaking Through the Constraining Regularities of Public School." *Environmental Education Research* 13, no. 2 (2007): 189–207.

———. "Place-Based Education." *International Handbook of Research on Environmental Education* (2013): 213.

Smith, Gregory A., and David Sobel. *Place- and Community-Based Education in Schools*. New York: Routledge, 2010.

Smith, Gregory A., and Dilafruz R. Williams. *Ecological Education in Action: On Weaving Education, Culture, and the Environment*. Albany, NY: State University of New York Press, 1999.

Snyder, Gary. *The Gary Snyder Reader: Prose, Poetry and Translations 1952–1998*. Washington: Counterpoint, 1999.

Stone, Michael K., and Zenobia Barlow, eds. *Ecological Literacy: Educating Our Children for a Sustainable World*. San Francisco: Sierra Club Books, 2005.

Strich, Dave. "Reflective Sit Spots." *Green Teacher* 95 (2012), 22–24.

Takahashi, Yuka. "Personal and Social Transformation: A Complementary Process Toward Ecological Consciousness." In *Learning Toward an Ecological Consciousness: Selected Transformative Practices*, edited by Edmund O'Sullivan and Marilyn M. Taylor, 169–182. New York: Palgrave Macmillan, 2004.

Tanner, Thomas. "Significant Life Experiences: A New Research Area in Environmental Education." *Journal of Environmental Education* 11, no. 4 (1980), 20–24.

Thoreau, Henry David. *Walden: A Writer's Edition*. New York: Holt, Rinehart and Winston, 1961.

Traina, Frank. "The Challenge of Bioregional Education." In *Perspectives in Bioregional Education*, edited by Frank Traina and Susan Darley-Hill, 19–26. Troy, OH: North American Association for Environmental Education, 1995.

Traina, Frank, and Susan Darley-Hill, eds. *Perspectives in Bioregional Education*. Troy, OH: North American Association for Environmental Education, 1995.

Tuan, Yi-Fu. *Man and Nature*. Washington: Association of American Geographers, Commission on College Geography, 1971.

———. *Space and Place: The Perspective of Experience*. Minneapolis: University of Minnesota Press, 1977.

Tyler, Ralph W. *Basic Principles of Curriculum and Instruction*. Chicago: University of Chicago Press, 1949.

Van Matre, Steve. *Acclimatizing: A Personal and Reflective Approach to a Natural Relationship*. Martinsville, IN: American Camping Association, 1974.

Webber, Elizabeth. "A School without Walls: Children Experience Place-based, Permaculture-inspired Waldorf Education in Portland's Mother Earth School." *LILIPOH* 18, no. 71 (2013): 28–33.

INDEX

collecting and organizing: introduction to, 37, 39; precipitation unit, 39–42; sunshine and temperature unit, 42–43; wind and air unit, 43–44

colour, 57–58, 76

Come on, Rain! (Hesse), 34

community, 25

concepts, catching, 80

context, change of, 37

Coombes School, 13

corpse (*Shavasana*) pose, 51

creative writing, 79, 80–81, 108

curricula, 11, 22. *See also* unit planning

D

dandelions vignette, 110

Deer's View activity, 91–93

detectives, change, 76–77

drama, *see* games, drama, and play

E

ecological education: changing the context for, 16; current approaches to, 15–16; focus on relationships in, 20–21; limits of current approaches to, 12–15; and place, 19; and technology, 16. *See also* Imaginative Ecological Education

ecological issues, 8–9, 10, 110–11

ecological monitors activity, 78

ecological understanding, 9–10, 12, 18, 19, 24. *See also* ecological education

Egan, Kieran, 17, 30, 49, 65, 66

Eisner, Elliot, 21

elementary grades, see primary and elementary grades

emotional response, 49, 53–54, 55

emotions, 18

empathy, 18. *See also* imagination

engagement, principles of, 21, 22, 61. *See also* activeness principle; feeling principle; place, sense of

Environmental School Project (Maple Ridge), 13, 26, 136n17

epiphytes, 97–98

Equinox Holistic Alternative School, 13

evaluation and assessment, 111, 113–14

extremes of experience/limits of reality, 36, 39, 42

F

feeling principle: and activeness principle, 59; aim of, 47; introduction to, 21, 22–23; tools for, 22; in unit planning, 126–27

field journal, 75

fire, 58

Forest Schools, 13, 14

forest soup, 95

fossils and geological features, 101–3

Franklin, Benjamin, 38

G

games, drama, and play, 31, 35

geological features and fossils, 101–3

gesture, 49

Greek mythology, 34, 55, 56–57

Green Teacher (magazine), 15

H

heroes, local, 75–76

heroic qualities, 36, 37–38

Hesse, Karen: *Come on, Rain!*, 34

Hill, Allen, 14

Hoadley, David, 38

hobbies, 37. *See also* collecting and organizing

Homer, 22

"Honouring" activities, 50, 55–56, 111

Hughes, Ted: "Wind," 56

humanizing meaning, 36, 38–39

humour: and incongruity, 49, 54–55; and jokes, 30, 33

I

identification, 18. *See also* imagination

IEE, *see* Imaginative Ecological Education

imagination, 11, 17–18

Imaginative Ecological Education (IEE): administrative tips for starting, 116–17; central claim of, 29; components of, 15; emotional engagement in, 29; overview of, 10, 11, 121; pedagogical tips for starting, 115–16; personal tips for starting, 114–15; physical tools and resources for, 116–17; principles of, 21, 61; and relationships, 20–21; role of teachers in, 61; and sense of place, 25, 70; as "slow" pedagogy, 25; students viewed in, 17; unit planning, 126–28; as weaving, 21; and

place poems, 109

planning, *see* unit planning

plant studies, 76

play, *see* games, drama, and play

postcards, 79–80

precipitation unit, 39–42

primary and elementary grades: mythic story form for, 69–70; place-based activities for, 108–9; place-making activities for grades 3–7, 78–81; place-making activities for K–3, 75–78; tools for, 30–31. *See also* tracking I activities; tracking I and II activities

Project Wild, 15

puzzle and mystery, 31, 34–35

R

rabbit ears game, 100

rain, 41, 53, 56, 57

Rain Drop Splash (Tresselt), 34

reality, *see* extremes of experience/limits of reality

recycling, 8, 10

relational pedagogy, 20

rhyme, rhythm, and pattern, 31, 34

rituals, shared, 62

riverbed activities: approach to, 101; calls, 106; fossils and geological features, 101–3; soundscapes, 107–8; walking upstream, 104–6; water activities, 103–4

riverside activities: animoves, 88–89; approach to, 82–83; casting a spell, 83–85; finding and keeping tracks, 85–86; water activities, 86–87

role play, 37

Roman mythology, 34

romantic story form, 70

romantic understanding (written language): introduction to, 30; teaching template for, 119–20, 124–25; tools for, 22, 36–37; in tracking II activities, 82

S

Saturna Ecological Education Centre (SEEC), 13

Schafer, R. Murray, 107

Sea-to-Sky Outdoor School for Sustainability Education, 16

secondary grades, *see* middle and secondary grades

senses, 49, 53, 54, 93–95

sensory training, 77–78, 138n4

shadows, 57, 79

Shadow Wolves, 73

Shavasana (corpse) pose, 51

sight, 93

sleeping miser game, 100

smell, 93–94

somatic understanding, 29, 48, 49. *See also* body's tools

songlines, 109

sound, 93

soundmarks, 107

soundscapes, 107–8

sound signals, 107

spell, casting a, 83–85

SPOT activity, 62–63, 65

stalking, 99–101

stillness, 50

storm chasing, 38

story form, 22–23, 30, 31–32, 42–43, 127

sun, 57

Sunnyside Environmental (Middle) School, 13

sunshine and temperature unit, 42–43

Swift, Jonathan, 32–33

T

Tadasana (mountain) pose, 50–51

taste, 94

teachers: own engagement of IEE principles, 25–26, 115; role in IEE, 61; and sense of place, 25, 70, 115, 116

teaching, 17–18, 21, 115

Teaching Green (Grant and Littlejohn), 134n1

technology, 16

temperature and sunshine unit, 42–43

templates: approach to, 117, 120; cognitive tools tables, 132–33; mythic planning, 117–18, 122–23; romantic planning, 119–20, 124–25; teaching overview table, 130; unit overview table, 131. *See also* unit planning

touch, 94

tracking, 68, 69, 73–74. *See also* literacy unit

tracking guides, 109

tracking I activities: animoves, 88–89; approach to, 82; branches, 97; finding and keeping tracks, 85, 90–91; tree story, 95–96; walking upstream, 104–5; water activities, 86